Vodka-flavored Tears

Vodka-flavored Tears

True Stories of a Misspent Youth

Timothy J. Hillegonds

www.timhillegonds.com

Cover design by Jon Wenzel

ISBN 978-0-615-40624-4

For Haley Jade

Some names have been changed.

Contents

x

Acknowledgements

It's hard to know where to begin when I think about all the people that have helped me along the way. Every story in this book would have been impossible to write without those of you that helped me see my way through. Thank you to my parents for continuing to go to bat for me, even when I didn't deserve it. To Richie and Dan: some bonds will never be broken and I am forever in your debt. Thank you to Wayne for helping pick me up when I fell, to Andrea for the plane ticket and so many other things, to Nick D. for being the most creative dude I know and never letting the dream die, and to Kevin, Stens, Beez, Jimmy, Mary, and E for playing such major roles in my life. To Heidi, Aaron, and Jillian: thank you for continuing to love me even though I was broken—your big brother is back. To those of you who appeared in these stories that I haven't already mentioned, thanks for the memories. I am forever grateful to Kevin Cunningham for showing me there was an easier, softer way. And to Haley Jade: the road is rough, but it is long, and someday we will dance.

Introduction

*"Given the choice between the experience of
pain and nothing, I would choose pain."*

William Faulkner

In the winter of 1996, as Father Christmas stood at the doorstep of Chicago readying himself to make his yearly visit to the Windy City, I boarded a plane with a bag of clothes, a hundred dollars, a snowboard, and the desire to leave my life I as I knew it and not look back. Years of flying the rebel flag of adolescence had left a wake of broken relationships and court dates behind me, and the only solace I seemed to be able to find was at the bottom of a clear bottle. But the problem with liquid consolation isn't that it doesn't work or it isn't effective, it's that it paves the road to perdition with broken glass. It does a beautiful job of anesthetizing the pain that one feels for a time, but it causes the already flawed judgment of the American teenager to become infected even more. So, at eighteen years old, while the tears of my mother slowly fell upon a certain Southside sidewalk, I flew west to lose myself in the snowcapped peaks of the Rocky Mountains.

I arrived in Colorado on December 25th, 1996, and by early 1997 I was a certified member of what parents all across the world refer to as "the wrong crowd." I was a few months into what would later hail to be the absolutely most destructive relationship of my life, and my plan to escape the troubles that plagued me in Chicago had failed in epic proportions. I was hurt. I was angry. I was James Dean in a Porsche 550 Spyder driving head on towards Donald Turnupseed.

The decisions that I made at that point in my life weren't so much decisions as they were emotional reactions to the rising sun of each new day. I was always cognizant of what the ramifications of my actions would be, but I couldn't seem to locate the heartstring I needed to pull to make myself care.

In 1997, at nineteen years old, two life changing things occurred for me: my girlfriend became pregnant, and I was charged with a felony. I'll talk about the felony first.

After drinking a bottle of vodka and consuming a midmorning snack consisting entirely of Vicodin, I got in a car in an attempt to get away from another episodic argument with my then pregnant girlfriend. I drove fast and thought slow, and before I knew it, I saw the pulsating reds and blues of the local black and white behind me. I slowed the car and pulled over. I watched with a growing rage as the sheriff approached my vehicle. Everything I hated in my life at the time flashed across the movie screen inside my head. I was a nineteen year old drop out with a pregnant girlfriend, an absent father, and a long list of sorrys I needed to say. I hated myself and my life and the cop that was approaching my car with an unbridled passion, and in an instant that would alter my life irrevocably, I slammed my foot on the gas pedal.

The insanity that ensued over the course of the next few minutes ended with me in the rear seat of a police car with my hands cuffed behind my back, staring at the smoking wreckage of the car that I was driving. And it was oddly ironic. I had idolized James Dean for the greater part of my short lived existence and in many ways was so much like him. But there I was, unlike my idol, walking away from a car wreck that could have killed me. I had, essentially, followed him to the exit gates of mortality, but been spared from passing through.

I ended up being charged with a felony and my lack of proper funding had me seeking counsel through the state appointed attorney. He was a good guy in a bad suit with a jam packed caseload and he advised me to agree to the plea bargain the state was giving me: plead guilty to the felony in exchange for dismissing a few of the other charges.

It was bad advice, but I took it anyway. I suppose I really had no other options. My life had been irrevocably altered.

In the winter that followed the summer I picked up the felony, in January of 1998, my girlfriend gave birth to my daughter. I was scared to death. I was a fucking train wreck of a person, a lost little boy with a mounting addiction to cocaine and vodka that couldn't cope with the reality of his own life, let alone that of a little girl.

But I tried to make it work.

I tried to work towards a future with her mother, hoping that a strong resolve would be enough to push us through to better times.

Ultimately, it wasn't. We fought. A lot. And I couldn't seem to stay out of jail long enough to begin to pick up the pieces of my broken life. I drank. I did drugs. I hurt myself in ways I couldn't even comprehend at the time. And when the shoe had finally dropped, I had to make a choice. Leave Colorado. Leave my daughter. Or end up doing hard time. Real time. Prison as opposed to jail time.

I stayed for a while, not being able to bear the thought of saying goodbye to Haley, but eventually I had no choice but to leave and head back to the Windy City, a city that I had missed with each beat of my heart since I left it. I left Colorado on a bus with a devastatingly broken heart, listening to soft cries of my beautiful daughter fading in the distance.

When I finally made it back to Chicago in the year 2000 I had to deal with the repercussions of the legal problems I had left behind when I fled a few years earlier. I had a couple of warrants and needed to take care of them before I could begin piecing my life back together. But it's hard to piece one's life back together when one's heart is broken into a million little fragments. I missed Haley and it hurt every second of everyday.

So I drank.

And did drugs.

And did everything I could to try and stop the pain I was feeling. I couldn't go back to Colorado because I had agreed to a plea bargain that stipulated I had to leave the state in exchange for a guilty plea and no more jail time. I had longed to get away from the tornado of an existence I had in Colorado, but I never knew it would come at such a heartbreaking expense.

Over the next five years, I fell in love, got engaged, fueled my addictions, lost the girl I loved, and did almost nothing to rectify my situation with Haley. I did my best to lose myself in the lights of the city I loved so much, and tried to drink and snort myself into a place where I would be able to finally face myself in the mirror.

In January of 2005, I got on a plane and flew to a rehabilitation center in the desolate cold of central Minnesota. I was twenty-six years old. I had a daughter that I hadn't seen in five years. And I was trying to figure out how I would be able to live my life when I could no longer live my life the only way that I knew how.

I stayed for twenty-eight days and when I left, I was different. I didn't know how I was different or why I was different, but I knew

I was different. But different is hard. Different is terrifying. Different is what happens when you face your demons and make a decision to change what you know, into what you *want* to know.

In the early days of sobriety I spent most of my time apologizing to all of the people I had let down and was doing my best to navigate through an existence no longer fueled by vodka and cocaine. I had a little girl I desperately needed to reconnect with and a spider web of legal problems that I needed to untangle. I was broken and angry and sad.

I wrote every day, begging for forgiveness by exposing each part of who I was unto the all seeing eyes of the internet. I wrote a blog and people read it and they helped me process the transition from the boy that I was into the man that I was hoping to be. They gave me strength and courage and hope, but most of all they gave me affirmation that I was doing the right thing.

I wrote everyday for a year while I struggled to stay sober. I wrote everyday for a year while I struggled to figure out where, exactly, I had lost my way. And that's where this book came from.

The stories I've written aren't special and they're not amazing and some of them aren't even stories, rather thoughts, but they do put a framework around my life. They've helped me tap into a childhood that I thought I had lost, one that I didn't even know I missed until I got sober. In most ways, I'm probably just like you. I'm an ordinary boy living in an extraordinary world that lost his way and is desperately trying to find it again.

Thank you for helping me.

Prologue

"The key to immortality is living a life worth remembering."

Bruce Lee

I remember.

At three years old my biological father left me and I lost my very first battle with alcohol.

When I was twelve, my mother began having flashbacks from years of abuse that she had suffered at the hand of her father, and was medicated to stabilize her moods. She hurt and cried and yelled and screamed and I didn't know what was happening. Childhood was over and I felt anger and vehemence exponentially. I had no money, my allowance was slim to none, and I got a job at a pet store.

Later that year, I was arrested for the first time.

By thirteen my mom had to plead to with the school to allow me to remain a student and by fourteen I hated anyone with a badge, a baton, or a bad attitude with ferocity. By fourteen I hung out with the Marlboro man on a consistent basis, and at fifteen I rolled my first blunt and fell in love with the way alcohol made me feel.

By sixteen years old I was in line skating professionally on a local stunt team, and when I was seventeen years of age I was kicked out of high school.

When I was eighteen years old I tried cocaine for the first time.

On Christmas day of my eighteenth year, with a hundred dollars to my name, I packed a bag of clothes and a snowboard, and bought a one way ticket west to live life the way that I always had.

Recklessly.

At nineteen I smoked crystal methamphetamine out of a light bulb and was immediately hooked. I smoked as much as I could as often as I could and would stay up for five days at a time.

By the end of my nineteenth year I had a daughter.

By twenty I was a convicted felon with a lengthy rap sheet and had already served two months in jail.

By twenty one years of age I had a gun, a vendetta, and three warrants spanning two states.

At the end of my twenty-first year, I moved back to Chicago and began to rebuild my life. I surrendered to the authorities, got a lawyer, went to court, paid my debt to society and began to change my ways.

At twenty two I got my G.E.D. and began to take college classes. I became engaged to a girl I wanted to marry with all my heart. I loved her with all that I was and all that I could be. I loved her at night and I loved her in the morning and I loved her with everything I had.

Her dad was a judge and he looked up my rap sheet and she was forbidden from seeing me but she didn't care and neither did I. We listened to rap music and screamed *"Fuck the world!"* at the top of our lungs and we loved each other completely.

At twenty-three I was a full blown alcoholic.

At twenty-four I did mountains of cocaine.

At twenty five the girl I loved left me for someone else. I missed her so much that it hurt to breathe.

At twenty six I drank as much as I could as often as I could and did cocaine until I felt like nothing could hurt me anymore. I hated myself and my life and everything that came with it.

At the end of my twenty-sixth year I went to a rehabilitation center in the middle of Minnesota.

At twenty-seven, two months before my twenty-eighth birthday, I am sober.

Vodka-flavored Tears

Nobody saves America by sniffing cocaine.
Jiggling your knees blank eyed in the rain,
when it snows in your nose you catch cold in your brain.

Allen Ginsberg

It was the third week of January in Chicago and the bitter cold numbness I felt went far beyond the icy grasp of winter. I had been spending most of my time in places lit up by neon or candles, trying to warm my insides with libations made from barley, hops, and the occasional potato. A year had passed since my relationship with my fiancé, Suzie, had ended but I still missed her with every fiber of my being. She had been a stamp of validation for me; proof that even though so many other things in my life had seemed to go so tragically wrong, that there was still a silver lining, a breath of fresh air to be found in a room full of life's toxic gases.

Every day seemed to run into the next. Tuesday became Thursday became Saturday became the next day. I awoke every morning to the same fucking thing, to the same routine. I would open my eyes in a room that was too bright, in a bed that was too hard, to an alarm clock that always went off too early. And then, inevitably, I would be late, going through every possible excuse I could come up with in order not to have to show up at a job I was all too fortunate to have in the first place. I would walk to the El train with my head throbbing, cursing myself for being hung over, for once again staying up until four in the morning while talking to a vodka-seven and snorting cocaine up my nose until I could no longer feel my teeth. I felt like I didn't live anymore. Like I just existed. Existed in a world in which the walls grew closer and closer together with the passing of each repetitive, tiresome day. I felt like I was slowly losing every piece of me that meant something. I had no pride anymore, no work ethic, no desire to go the extra mile or, on most days, even enter the race. I was employed solely to get a paycheck that I could use to buy a temporary fix. A forty bag would turn into an eight ball, and a few drinks down the street at the local hole in the wall would turn into an all night marathon.

Everything meant nothing and nothing meant everything.

Monday's dawn signified the birth of yet another premature workweek, and as the clock changed from 8:29 to 8:30, I found myself perched on the edge of an oversized red leather chair in the corner office on the twenty-ninth floor of the downtown Chicago skyscraper in which I was employed. I had sat in that chair on countless occasions, but this wasn't like all those other times. There were no smiles or laughter or dirty jokes being told through the cigar smoke that forever loomed in the office. This time was different. My heart pounded like bongos in my chest as I peered over the ten thousand dollar mahogany desk that separated me from the towering man that was my boss. I stared nervously into his eyes, the eyes of the man that had approached me almost two years ago while I was waiting tables at a local restaurant. He had, despite my criminal record and lack of education, given me a chance in the business world that someone like me normally wouldn't get. It was a rare opportunity; a chance to show that street sense and a tainted background just might prove to be a successful combination in business after all.

I knew what was coming.

He told me I had two choices; that I could resign immediately and he would give me thirty days severance pay, or he could fire me on the spot and I could collect unemployment. He told me he had a Chicago police officer waiting in the elevator bank, ready to arrest me if I decided to handle things in any way that was less than gentlemanly. He told me that he would press charges if things went south. He told me that I wasn't performing, or reforming, or conforming, or forming anything for that matter, that my attitude sucked, that I was late every day, and that he had no choice but to fire me.

He told me that and my eyes began to water because there was nothing I could say. I was the motherfucking epitome of failure. There were no words I could utter that could absolve me from truth that I wasn't who I said I was, that he was right, and the tightrope I had been trying to balance on had finally snapped.

So, I stood up and while tears threatened to breach the lids of my eyes, I thanked him, determined to leave with some sort of dignity. I went to my desk, got my bag, and walked to the elevator bank.

My inner dialogue had gone from a quiet whisper to a murderous scream, and as I hit the down button on the elevator wall, I tried to fight the monsoon of tears that was behind the slow drizzle that had already started. I screamed at myself in my head. Another day. Another epic failure. It was so typically me.

The mirrored elevator doors closed and I was forced to stare at myself. I looked tired, so absolutely beaten down that I was nearly unrecognizable. The rollercoaster ride I had been on for the last ten years of my life had finally broken down and all I was left with was a bad case of motion sickness. I was an abbreviated version of who I was supposed to be, a text message in place of an email because all of my qualities were lol.

Leaving the building I had been coming to for the last two years, I walked out into a bitter January wind that proceeded to slap me for being so fucking naïve. The sea of people flooding the streets of the busy Chicago Loop streamed past me in a dizzying display of unaffected oblivion. I began to sob. I sobbed because I had finally become the loser I had felt like for so long. I cried because my fiancé was gone, because I had no bank account and no money, because I hadn't paid a bill in almost a year and because my dry cleaning wasn't done. I cried because the one consistent thing I had, the one thing that brought some semblance of normalcy to the alcoholic whirlwind that had become my life was gone. I was furious at myself, a cynical mix of anger and defeat that had me yearning for one person, just one motherfucking person, to truly know how I felt.

I wanted to be back in Suzie's arms. I wanted her to tell me things would be alright and I would get through this and that she would continue to love me no matter how broken I was. I wanted to cry on her shoulder and finally admit to her that I wasn't happy, that I was so motherfucking far from happy. I wanted to tell her that I missed her so much and so badly that I had no desire to ever feel anything for anyone ever again. I wanted tell her I was sorry.

I just wanted to tell her I was sorry.

But she was gone, nothing but a bittersweet memory. A vague reminder that once upon a long time ago, I was good.

I called my friend Wayne, a friend to me in every sense of the word, and told him what happened. He listened in the way a good friend does and tried to find the right words to say in a situation in which nothing he could say would do. He told me to hang on, that he was going to come over, that we would talk and try to figure it out.

The wind blew.

I hung up my cell phone and wanted to get hit by a car. I wanted to walk in the middle of Franklin Avenue and start a fight with a Lincoln Navigator. I wanted to be hit so hard that some sense would finally find its way past my thick, thick skull. I wanted to be numb, to be still, to fall asleep and wake up in a place where I would never again feel this intolerable pain.

My cell phone rang. I put it to my ear, and the man who had just fired me began to talk. I listened. He told me that if I admitted I had a problem, if I was ready to admit that my life was completely and utterly unmanageable that he might have a solution. He told me that it wouldn't be easy, that it would be difficult and scary and full of hard fucking work. He said I would have to do it his way and no other way but if I did, if I manned up and stopped living a life driven by fear, that my life would get exponentially better.

My legs suddenly felt like they had battery acid in them. I leaned up against the wall of the Jones Lang LaSalle building and told him that I didn't know where to turn, that somewhere between my first drink and my last one I had been consumed by my habits.

He told me to go home, to wait for his next phone call, and to hold on. He told me that everything would be okay.

I hung up the phone, but everything was far from okay. I wanted cocaine. I wanted vodka. I wanted cocaine and vodka and a lot of it. I wanted to drink until I felt like me again. Like how I used to be. Like how I was before I knew better. I wanted to be me before I went to jail, me before I was kicked out of high school, me before I had a police record and a life altering felony. Me before my fiancé left me to start fucking the neighborhood tile setter, me before my dad walked out and left my mom and me to fend for ourselves. Me, when I was innocent.

I started to walk to the El and the felt an almost undeniable urge to bang my fucking head over and over against the walls of the stately buildings of downtown Chicago until I understood why I did the things I did. Why I was fearless in everything in my life, but absolutely scared to death right now. I wanted to understand how I could come so far only to end up in the same place. And God how I wanted to drink. I wanted to drink vodka and wine and beer and everything else I could get my hands on. I wanted to drink until I threw up and then I wanted to drink some more. I wanted to drink until being awake and asleep were the same. I wanted to drink until life was manageable and I didn't hate myself as much as I did right then.

I boarded the El and took the train through the city that I loved so much and thought about Suzie. I missed her smile, her laugh, her touch, her kiss. I missed looking in her eyes while I made love to her. I missed how she made me feel, how I didn't always have to be a soldier in front of her and I missed the brief moments with her in which I could let my guard down. I missed the drive she gave me, the way she made me want to conquer the world. I missed every word that I had ever written to her.

The train swayed and rocked and my thoughts turned to the letter I wrote her after we said our goodbyes.

I just got off the phone with you and finally realized that the thread of hope that I've been hanging onto was never really there in the first place. I don't know when you changed your mind and felt like you couldn't do this anymore, or exactly when I became something other than a priority in your life, or when this new relationship became more important than the friendship that we built together. But I do know a few things. I remember the future that you promised me, a future filled with more good times than bad, a future that ended up with a "happily ever after."

But now, it seems, that's no longer a possibility. My future, my friendship, my fiancé, my support, my stronghold, my reason to live to fight another day, has all been torn from my grasp and replaced with an empty spot in the bed where you used to sleep, an empty spot that holds a constant reminder of my failures as a partner as well as the faint aroma of Victoria Secret that's fading day by day. There is so much of me that still loves you more than Microsoft Word could ever begin to express...

I missed her because I loved her, but mostly I missed her because she was all I had. And right then, I needed her more than I needed the air that I breathed.

When the train stopped, the doors opened to let the wind slap me one more time. From the platform above Roosevelt Street I could see the icy waters of Lake Michigan glaring at me through the morning haze. I walked down the steps and continued down the road towards the condo I'd been living in with Rico. I deliberately stomped my feet to the ground harder and harder. I tried to feel something other than what I was feeling right then. I stomped. I screamed.

My heart ached.

I marched down to Michigan Avenue, but I had never been any less of a soldier. I was scared and afraid. I was hurt. I was angry. I was fucked up. I was in a hurry to get to the condo where I could drink something that would level me out.

I reached the doorway to the multi-million dollar high rise I lived in and realized I had been faking everything. I couldn't afford to live there. I didn't belong there. I may have had a doorman, but I hadn't paid my electric bill in eight months. I refused to check the mail because all it ever was were envelopes containing letters threatening litigation against me and bullshit junk mail.

I was bullshit junk mail.

I got into the elevator and rode it to the sixteenth floor where I got off and walked to the door of the half million dollar condo I called home and it dawned on me that I would never, ever own something that nice. My footsteps echoed off the walls because that place, like me, was hollow. It was a mask, a façade, a place to bring women to impress in hopes of finding out Victoria's secret. This was where I had chopped up line after line of cocaine rocks with an expired Bally's Gym membership card, a constant reminder of one more thing that I just couldn't finish.

I set down my bag, turned on the television and waited. I waited for something to happen, for anything to happen, for my phone to ring or the door to open or my heart to stop. I waited for clarity, but all I got was more fucking confusion.

There was a knock at the door and when it opened, Wayne walked in. I couldn't help but think that this was the first time that Wayne actually saw me for what I really was. The broken, tearstained, train wrecked person that stood before him was the real me and the real me was a mess. I was what was left in the wake of a tornado that danced with a hurricane. Bits and pieces of me were scattered all over different parts of the previous ten years and my infrastructure was finally failing.

Wayne looked at me and we started to talk. I told him that I didn't know what I was doing anymore, that the only meaning or purpose I found was in a clear bottle named after an abbreviated cuss word. I told him, while the tears began fall, that I was fucked up, that I was doing cocaine in large amounts and drinking until my body rejected it. I told him that I had a problem. He told me that he knew.

But he passed no judgment. He shook his head with sadness as I opened a bottle of wine, but said nothing. We stood on the balcony to smoke and as I drank, with each swallow, the warmth of the wine began to hug me, and life started to seem a little less bleak. I inhaled smoke and drank wine and listened as it lied to me, as it held me in its arms and began to fill me. I began to fill up with smoke and wine.

I was smoke and wine.

The ring of my cell phone cut through the smoky haze and I saw the familiar number to my office. My heart started to pound and I answered the phone with a shaky voice. It was the office manager, someone who had become a close friend of mine over the course of my employment. She had gone to bat for me a few times when I had dropped the ball, and I knew this whole situation was taking a toll on her as well. She told me how much she cared for me and how bad she wanted to help me. I said that I knew. She told me that my boss had instructed her to look into facilities to go to and that after she did, she found out that the insurance would only cover the kinds of places that got state aid. I imagined she was talking about places where crack addicts and heroin junkies talked about how many tricks they turned, and the beds smelled like feces and vomit.

But I didn't care. Anything was better than this.

She continued to tell me about a place in Minnesota where my boss had gone. A place that was supposedly tucked away on five hundred wooded acres and had hiking trails and its own little lake. She told me that if I was to go, if I was to make the decision to try and change my life, that I would have to do it 'in patient,' that I would get on a plane and fly to Minnesota for twenty eight days. She told me that the cost was $22,200.00 and that my boss would pay for it.

I took a drag from my cigarette and asked her when I would leave.

She told me that right now there were no open beds, but as soon as one became available, I would go. The facility was full most of the year and usually had a waiting list, but she and my boss would do their best to pull some strings to get me in as soon as they possibly could. She told me she needed to know what I wanted to do.

My thoughts drifted from the phone call as I came to the realization that I was at a defining moment in my life and I didn't know what to do. The smoke and wine had begun to numb the pain and my thoughts drifted to Rico. Rico was my roommate and my best friend and as my life was crumbling at a steady pace, he was oblivious to what was transpiring due to the fact that he was out of town. I knew that he was going to come home in a few days and I was going to have to tell him what was going on. I was going to have to tell him that the kid who didn't pick on him for being fat in elementary school had finally been defeated. I was going to have to tell him that I had tried my best to handle it all, but somewhere along the way I lost my grip and my life had been slowly slipping away from me ever since. I was going to have to tell him that I hadn't paid the cable or electric bill in months, and that I was going to cancel out of the cruise that we were about to go on.

I was going to have to tell him what a loser I had become.

I told the office manager that I would go and hung up the phone. I told Wayne I was going to rehab in Minnesota and I would be leaving soon. I looked out the window from the sixteenth floor and watched the Windy City blow snow back and forth across the balcony. I was overwhelmed by the decision I had made. The wine hugged me tighter and I decided that when Wayne left, I was going to do mountains of cocaine. I was going to do more cocaine that day than I had ever done before by myself and I was going to do it the minute Wayne left my house.

We talked for a bit more and it was time for Wayne to go.

He said goodbye and when the door shut behind him I was once again alone with my thoughts. I had two phone calls to make. One to my parents and one to my dealer.

My parents were first.

I picked up the phone and thought about what I was going to say to them. I was so fucking sick of having to make phone calls like this. I remembered what it was like to make that first collect phone call from my jail cell, to beg for money because for once in my life I really didn't want to sleep in the bed that I had made. I remember the sound of my mother's heart breaking. I remembered the sound of my step-fathers voice, the man who had voluntarily taken on the responsibility of raising me, the man that had tried so hard to teach me the meaning of integrity, honor, I remembered the sound of his voice when he said no.

I was a failure. A lost cause that took everything good and rotted it. I ruined birthdays, and mother's days and father's days and Christmases. I had a daughter and left her. I drank and fought and did crimes in the name of rebellion. And now, five years after the last colossal heartbreak, I was about to make another call. I was debris.

I looked at my cell phone and I wanted to throw it against the wall. I stared at the number zero because that's what I was. I was nothing. I was zero.

I dialed the phone number and my mom answered.

She asked me how I was and I told her I wasn't good.

She asked me what was wrong.

What I wanted to say and what I did say were two different things entirely. I wanted to tell my mom that I wished she had aborted me. I wanted to tell her that I was so sick and tired of being sick and tired that I just wanted to go to sleep and not wake up. I wanted to tell her that I was exhausted, that I couldn't possibly fathom living my life without vodka to sing me to sleep. I wanted to tell her that her son was a grade A fuck up and that I was so sorry, so motherfucking sorry for not being a better one. I wanted to tell her that I loved her and that it wasn't her fault, that she had done what she could, that I knew she and dad had tried their best to raise me right but I was determined to give everything and everyone the middle finger. I just wanted my mom to know that there were times in my life when I tried so hard, times when I missed her so much. I just wanted to tell her I was sorry.

I told her I was going to rehab.

(Panic.)

She asked me what for.

(More panic.)

I told her it was because I drank so much, so often that I had panic attacks when I wasn't drinking enough. I told her it was because I snorted cocaine as much and as often as I could, and there was no way I could stand living like that any longer.

She was silent. Then she whispered my name.

That was all she said but it was enough to build an internal scream I could feel in my bones. I felt anger and rage rush through my body in a tidal wave of fury. I wanted to tell her that I hated myself for everything I was and for everything I wasn't. I wanted to tell her that it hurt so bad that I just didn't give a fuck about anything anymore.

But instead, through the deafening silence between the phones, I listened to my moms heart breaking again. And when she was finished saying what she had to say, I told her about where I was going and that things were going to be okay. I told her because she needed to hear it, that even though I didn't believe a word that was coming out of my mouth, she needed to hear it and maybe, just maybe, I did too.

A few minutes later I hung up the phone and went to my room to change clothes. I passed the full length mirror on the wall and once again saw my reflection. I looked tired and beaten up. I looked hungover. I had the look of addiction in my empty eyes.

I picked up the phone again and called my coke dealer.

I lived in an area of Chicago that had been undergoing gentrification. The South Loop of ten years ago was gone for the most part, and the seedy warehouses and buildings that it was made up of a decade ago were replaced with newly rehabbed condos and luxury high-rise living. But only blocks away from the lavishness I had surrounded myself with stood a tall building that still catered to the Section 8 crowd. My coke dealer was a true hustler, a man that had gone through his life with nothing but hustles and cons and was constantly one step away from life inside a correctional facility. He answered the phone on the third ring and I told him I was going to be over in a little bit. He told me he was making some stops, but he would have his girlfriend meet me.

I threw on a jacket and caught a cab to the parking lot of his building and I walked into the front door and checked in with security. The security guard probably knew why I was there, he probably knew why almost all of the white people were there, but I didn't care. I signed in and called up to her and she invited me in to wait until my dealer got back.

The elevator creaked while it struggled to climb to the floor that housed the small one bedroom apartment they lived in. I had been there once before a few months back and remembered it was filled with mismatched and broken furniture and smelled musty, like old shoes. It reeked of stale Newport cigarettes and was littered with empty green and white boxes. But it was perfect for me. Because I wanted to be in shitty apartment in a shitty, a poverty ridden building, with my shitty coke dealer's girlfriend and my shitty, fucked up self. It was where I felt like I belonged. It was shitty. I was shitty.

I knocked on her door and two minutes and two hundred dollars later I was emptying rocks from a small baggy onto a plate she had gotten me from the kitchen. I began crushing them with my CTA card and arranging them into John Gotti sized lines in front of me. I rolled up a twenty-dollar bill, put the end to my nose, and inhaled until my problems disappeared. I coughed, swallowed, and did it again. I was once again ready to believe my own sweet lies.

I always believed that I was one deep inhalation away from figuring out what was wrong with me. I always believed that I just didn't have the right combo, that if I added a little more vodka and a little less coke, or not so much Ecstasy and a Vicodin or two, that everything would be okay. But this time, as my synthetic fantasy raged, part of me believed that if I made it through the next week or so alive, that it would all be over. There was a certain comfort in knowing I was going to rehab. Amidst all of the emotions and thoughts whirling inside my skull there was a nagging feeling of gladness that I'd finally be put on a plane and given the chance to stop. I believed that I could (sniff) do this.

I spent the next hour or so inhaling coke, licking the card I was using to cut up the lines, talking to my dealer's girlfriend, and waiting for the phone call my boss had promised to give me. I was scared to talk to him though, scared that he would see right through me, that he would hear the music that was playing in the background, identify my stuffed up nose, and figure out what I was doing. When he eventually called, we talked for about ten minutes. He told me what it would be like in rehab (he had been there), about some of his experiences, and he told me that it was the best thing he had ever done in his life. He said that I would learn gimmicky sayings and see a plethora of acronyms that would be used to help me remember some of the important concepts. He said I would be expected to talk a lot. He told me that one of the things that had stuck out to him was the acronym *H.O.W.* It stood for honesty, openness and willingness. He talked and my mind registered the irony of the situation. It registered how ridiculously ironic that acronym was at that precise moment. Because right then I couldn't have been further from honest or open. Honesty would have been telling him that I was in the first stages of a bender and I didn't know when it would end. Being open would have been me telling him that I was doing coke so fast and so often it was falling out of my nose and I couldn't fucking see straight. Being willing, well, being willing was something I was and something I told him. I was willing. I wanted this to be over. Here, now, in the middle of a drug and alcohol fueled bender I knew that this was not how I wanted to live. I was in a Section 8 housing complex snorting cocaine with the twenty three year old girlfriend of my forty-five year old coke dealer with a sleeping two year old in the next room, talking to the man who had fired me only hours earlier.

My life was complete insanity.

We finished up our conversation and I put the phone in my pocket and went back to my plate. A quick sniff and I finished what I had lined up, and went downstairs to meet my dealer who had just arrived. He showed me the new Ford Five Hundred he had just bought and asked me if I wanted to ride with him while he made a few stops. I did this sometimes, riding around the neighborhood passing out little baggies of cocaine to people from all walks of life, from guys in business suits to soccer moms to frat boys. But this time I told him I just wanted to head home. I told him the abbreviated version of what had happened and he told me he was sorry and to call him later if I needed him.

I told him I would.

He drove me to where I lived and I got out of the car in front of the place that would never be my home and went upstairs to do more cocaine. My thoughts zigged and zagged, going from one thing to the next, then back again. I was once again alone with my thoughts and choices and I began to chop up lines.

My jaw was clenched, involuntarily forcing my teeth together, while I once more transformed rocks into powder. I scraped them into four big lines and sucked until what was four, was three. My heart beat outside of my chest, but the desire to do more raged like an unquenchable thirst. I was no longer human, I was product defect. I was rapid heartbeats and beaded sweat.

I was madness.

I thought about the day my daughter was born. How I watched in awe and wonderment as new life began its journey. I remembered how I watched as the product of lust and love took the female form and cried out in pain, surprise, and shock when the first sensations of this cold world enveloped her skin in the form of frigid, hospital air. She was it. The secret of life. She was the majestic twinkle of an eye, but I blinked and she was gone.

I shook my head but all it did was blur my vision.

I turned on the television and saw static and heard noise. Nobody was talking but everybody was talking and I couldn't concentrate on anything. I was a mass of confusion in need of a Marlboro Light. The wind blew, the snow fell, I snorted coke, and the monotony of what my life had become continued.

Hours later, when the coke was finally gone, I lay on my black leather couch and listened to my heartbeat. My mind raced, but time stood still, and I knew that in one more week I'd be done. Rehab scared me. I didn't know how to walk without my crutches and what I was about to do seemed insurmountable.

I wondered if I would die.

I wondered if I had pushed myself too far. I tried to slow my mind, to dull my thoughts, but they were jagged and obtuse and slicing my soul to pieces.

The darkness of the night moved over to make way for dawn and sometime, with time and space slow dancing to the sound of my broken heart, I fell asleep.

I slept most of that day and part of the rest and sometime throughout, Rico came home. I told him that I was going to rehab and that I'd be gone for a month. I told him I was done, that I had danced with the devil for far too long and that it was time the music stopped. And this time, when I said the words, I knew that I meant it and I was not going to fail. Rico had my back like he always did, and told me that everything would be cool. I smiled and told him that I hoped so.

The Thursday before the Friday I was to leave, I went out to dinner with a girl. I ordered a glass of red wine and slowly sipped the last drink my lips would ever taste. I talked with my friend over dinner, but my heart and mind were in other places. I got up to go to the bathroom and called my dealer. I told him to meet me at the house with one last forty bag and he told me he'd be there in a little while. I went back to the table, finished my dinner, took a long look at the last sip of wine I would ever drink and poured it down my throat. I paid the check and we left for my house.

As we drove back through the city I lost myself in its lights and wished with all my heart that tomorrow would never come. That night felt like the last night I would be me. I knew drinking. I knew cocaine. I knew drug dealers, criminals, and fuck ups. I knew jail cells and I knew manipulation. I didn't know rehab.

I volleyed wanting to go and not wanting to go back in forth in my head. My birthday was in two months, how was I going to not drink? What about my wedding day? What about anybody's wedding day? What about Fridays, fuck it, what about Saturday, Sunday and every other goddamn day that I was supposed to live without vodka? How was I supposed to live in this shitty, fucked, up life completely sober?

My dealer was waiting at my place when I got there and we talked for a little while. I told him that I didn't know when I would see him again and he told me he understood. He said that he wouldn't just miss the money, and that I was a good kid and would figure it out. I thought about what he said and about what he did for a living and realized that he wasn't a bad guy, he was just the doctor with the prescription I needed filled. We said goodbye and I rode the elevator up to the condo with the last bag of coke I would ever do.

Once upstairs, I chopped the rocks into two monster lines and inhaled one line in each nostril. The feeling hit me like a knockout punch and my heart beat like an African drum. I sat on the couch and turned on the TV and, before I knew it, the feeling had passed. I fell asleep.

I got up the next morning and flew to Minnesota to see a guy about a thing. I didn't know what I was doing or even how I was going to do it but in the back of my mind I knew that that was probably the plane ride that would save my life. I was finally going to have to face the man in the mirror and fight that motherfucker head to head.

The plane rose higher and higher into the gray sky and I looked out the window at the world below. So much had changed in the previous week and everything seemed like a dream. I didn't know what was going to happen when the plane landed. I didn't know how I would feel or what I would go through but right then, as I flew above the clouds, I was sad. My eyes welled up and I blinked, causing a tear to run down my cheek and onto my quivering lip.

It tasted like vodka.

Through the Rear View

"Adults are just obsolete children and the hell with them."

Dr. Seuss

Once upon a long time ago, things were so much simpler. *Business casual* was a term reserved for your friends' parents and days were over by 3:15. Practice was mandatory, exercise was fun, and lunch, complete with desert and a carton of milk, was less than three dollars. *Nine eleven* referred to wing sauce at Hooters, cigarettes were only bad if you got caught smoking them, and alcohol still had an air of mystery to it. Heartache and romance began and ended with a handwritten note in which the *I's* were dotted with hearts, and nothing could top the feeling from the day that you heard that she said that you two might be good together.

Saturdays started out on a skateboard and ended up at a bonfire while church interrupted every Sunday morning. Religion wasn't yet a choice, most prayers started out with, "God, if you give me this one thing, I promise to never...," and death was something that only happened to old people.

Will Smith rapped the theme song to our lives and Marky Mark had a funky bunch. Eminem was just a candy, Compton didn't exist outside of our television screens, and Ice Cube was just a boy in the hood. The girls rocked white Keds® and I.O.U.® sweatshirts while the boys flossed Z. Cavaricci® and some B.U.M Equipment®. Low top shoes were obsolete, colors were hyper, and silk shirts dominated the dance floor.

We learned how to deal with problems on after school specials and learned about sex and drugs from 90210. Wayne had a world, Bill and Ted had an adventure, and we went back to the future three times.

Minimum wage was doable and work weeks were six hours long. We were limited by our allowance, but it didn't matter because just hanging out didn't cost a whole lot. We couldn't buy time because it was freely given, and friendship was our biggest responsibility.

We traveled down the yellow brick road, through the poppy field, and somewhere along the way we took a little nap because we were oh, so tired. And that's when it happened.

Life.

When we woke, the yellow brick road was paved into an expressway, and the poppy field had been turned into a subdivision. We looked around flustered, muttered a curse word, and got in the car. Gathering speed, we merged into the fast lane, glancing in the rear view one last time.

Damn.

Somewhere in Middle America

*"When I was a kid I used to pray every night for a new bicycle.
Then I realized that the Lord doesn't work that way so
I stole one and asked Him to forgive me."*

Emo Phillips

When I was seventeen years old, due to a school board vote, I was kicked out of high school. My endless pranks and constant disregard for anything involving an authoritative figure had finally pushed the "powers that be" into making a decision. The rubber was finally meeting the road, and although I didn't realize it at the time, that monumental decision would leave a tread mark on me that I would feel long into my uncertain future. That decision changed me though, molded me, taught me lessons that I wouldn't comprehend until years later.

Even today, at times when life seems to be getting the upper hand, I find myself thinking that back to that moment, to that one instant where everything I knew veered dangerously off course. I play the *What If* game. What if I hadn't left? What if I'd tried harder? What if I had just not given up?

But the *What If* game is unsatisfying at best. It brings no closure or restitution or alleviation. It only causes me to peek back in time, into closets where skeletons hang that are probably best left alone.

It was fall on Chicago's Southwest side and the leaves were changing. The winds brought promises of another Midwest winter and as they blew autumn colored leaves across the streets outside my high school, I found myself walking the halls alone in my thoughts. It was another typical day in a typical school with typically damaged teenagers trying to steer through the perilous pathways of adolescence. I was hurting that day; hurting for reasons I wasn't ready to come to terms with. I was thinking about my life and the way that I felt about it, trying my best to control the mounting anger that seemed to follow me everywhere that I went. I was on the edge of control, balancing in the no man's land that lies between what's right and what's wrong.

While I was walking and thinking, one of the other kids came up to me and asked me if I was planning on skipping my next class. I don't remember who it was or why he said it, just that he did. I remember thinking that I *wasn't* going to skip class that day. I remember thinking that I was going to continue walking down that corridor into my next classroom, sit down in my seat, and do my best to learn whatever it was that was being taught. But when that kid asked me that question everything changed.

I stopped walking and looked at him.

And I nodded my head ever so slightly.

"Yeah, fuck this. I'm leaving."

To this day I don't know why I did that, why I said that I was going to leave when I had absolutely no intention of doing so. But when that kid looked at me and asked that question, the ever present sick feeling in my stomach clawed at my insides and something inside of me broke. I hated my life. I hated the fact that my dad had walked out on my mom and me so many years before, and I hated that I couldn't block it out any longer. I hated that I had spent the greater part of my seventeen years chasing something I could never see or hold or grasp, like I was chasing a mirage. I was looking for the Statue of Liberty right after David Copperfield had made it disappear. I was trying to be an island on the outside when on the inside I was housing an entire continent of sadness. I desperately wanted someone to show me how to fix my life, how to live it, how to make peace with the demons that haunted my every atom.

Looking back on that day, I know that a part of me realized that if I left, it would all be over, and whatever bit of adolescence I had been hanging onto would be gone. When I stepped foot on the other side of those school doors, I wouldn't be let back in and I would be standing at the beginning of a road I would walk alone.

On that day, in that hallway, I looked around one last time and walked to the doors that led to the parking lot. It had been a good run for me, or so I thought, a valiant effort. But it was time to go. I didn't belong there and I couldn't fake it any longer.

I walked across the parking lot where I would never park again, glanced in the direction of the school to the bushes where I used to smoke in between classes, and unlocked my car. I looked at the school with a mixture of contempt, confusion, sadness and loss, half hoping someone would come out to stop me.

But no one did.

I knew that I couldn't keep doing what I was doing, and that I couldn't continue to go to a school that either didn't understand me or wouldn't try. I knew that I had to make a decision. Stay or go. I knew that I would have to make that decision even if doing so would alter the rest of my life and trigger a sequence of events that would bring a thunderstorm of shame, regret, and eventually remorse.

I got in my car, shut the door, started it up, and as the car lit up with power, the Counting Crows song *Omaha* poured out of the speakers. I backed out of my spot, switched into drive, and slowly drove into the hardest years of my life.

The words of that song still ring in my ears.

Omaha, somewhere in Middle America
Getting right to the heart of matters
It's the heart that matters more
I think you better turn your ticket in and
get your money back at the door

The Break In

*"Perhaps the world's second worst crime is boredom.
The first is being a bore."*

Jean Baudrillard

In 1991, while Boris Yelsten was becoming the first freely elected president of Russia, I was a seventh grader in America doing something I felt was equally important: I was committing my first B&E. And while it's true that I was young, I felt that thirteen was high time to devote myself to a specific area of the criminal craft. I had dabbled in theft when I was twelve, but found out rather quickly that I was no match for the technological advancements of the twentieth century. It wasn't that my attempts at stealing every present I planned on giving at Christmas that year were unplanned or not well thought out, it was just that when stores started sticking electronic sensors inside the items I planned on stealing, it required that I posess deactivation devices that my non-existent allowance couldn't cover. I did well for a little while though, strategically removing the stick on sensors from compact discs and bottles of Aspen cologne. It was only when we, or should I say I, as to not incriminate my cohorts, decided to try bigger ticket items like mom's new hairdryer and dad's Hilti hammer drill, that the long arm of the law reached out and strangled me.

It was pretty obvious to me at that stage of my life that petty theft was not my forte. If I had aspirations of attaining an iconic status as a criminal I was going to have to branch out and try some new things.

So, as it was, burglary seemed like a much safer bet. With no people around during the actual committing of the crime the chances that I would be caught were significantly less. But that wasn't the only advantage though, there was also the James Dean factor that true cat burglars possessed, what I viewed as a distinguished "coolness." Cat burglars didn't have to be violent brutes that carried out heinous crimes while civil society slept. Instead, they could be charismatic and debonair.

They could have strong English accents and rugged good looks – think Sean Connery in the movie *Entrapment*. They could romance the ladies with their sophisticated guise and well spoken demeanor. Yes, at thirteen years old, I had decided to be a burglar.

My previous round of crime and punishment had left me weary and contemplating the need for a partner. My Old Man had always referred to my friends as "my partners in crime" and I realized that maybe he was on to something. Maybe what I was missing was an accomplice. The way I saw it, and I saw things in some pretty obscure ways back then, having an accomplice did two things for me: one good, one bad. The bad thing, what I knew to be called the con (no pun intended), was that whatever ill-gotten gains I happened to come across during my adventure would have to be split according to how many accomplices I had. It wasn't that I was greedy, it was just that my yearly earnings in the seventh grade totaled somewhere around thirty-five dollars, and that included my birthday money. So if our criminal mischief revealed a treasure of, say, ten dollars, that meant that I boosted my annual net worth by almost thirty percent, hardly a small feat when you consider the numbers. Having to split that two or three ways was almost incomprehensible. But the upside, the pro as it's called, was that there's strength and safety in numbers. If I got caught, and that was definitely a possibility, it was better to be caught with my friends.

So I decided to have an accomplice. Batman had Robin, Bonnie had Clyde, even the Fresh Prince had Jazzy Jeff so why shouldn't I, a young man with aspirations that were easily as great as any of those people, have one too?

My best friend was a kid named Richie D., pronounced *Richiedee*, who lived a little further south of Chicago than I did. And since childhood friends are essentially picked according to the geographic location their neighborhood falls into, it was sort of an anomaly that we were friends at all. His neighborhood was ten miles or so away, almost a light year in kid distance, but since we were both born into the Dutch Christian Reformed tradition, we attended the same small, parochial elementary school.

Richie D. had a younger sister named Red that had somehow breached the force field that all brothers put up so as not to have to hang out with their younger sibling. I never minded it, though, because Red was one of those girls that was just one of the guys—at least until she became my first kiss later that year whereas she immediately went from "just one of the guys" to "Sloppy Joe." (Author's note: I still maintain that the originator of the nickname was not me, rather, it was the brainchild of Kyle Osterman. Therefore, with all things being considered equally, I should be freed of the resentment Red has been harboring for the last twenty years.)

Red was skinny and athletic with pale, freckled skin and vibrant red hair. And she was loud. And by loud I mean loud like boys are supposed to be loud. Pissing off Red was absolutely one of the worst things to do because it was only a matter of time before everyone, and by everyone I mean *everyone*, including the aboriginal people of the Australian outback, could hear her yelling at you.

Richie D. and Red had a grandmother that lived in the same neighborhood as me so a few times a month they would come for a visit and it would be open season for those of us that thought mischief was a sport. We would get together and hang out and spend sunny afternoons in-line skating in front of the bungalows, ranches, and neo-eclectic houses that made up most of Chicago's South side. It was right about that time that in-line skating was venturing forward into mainstream culture from its roots as a way for hockey players to train in the summer. It was becoming more commonplace to see people skating awkwardly down sidewalks, the fear of falling radiating from their wrinkled brows and outstretched arms. There was even a tale circulating through the rumor mills of a man that had somehow rigged a fan to his back powered by a lawn mower engine that allowed him to reach speeds of epic proportions. "A hundred miles an hour!" some kids said. We never saw the guy, but he was a hero in our minds, a modern day Einstein using science to shatter nature's laws and the city's motorized vehicle safety regulations as he pushed the limits of rebellion.

Earlier in the year I had sweet talked my grandmother into buying me a pair of skates, but they seemed to be lacking in the "smoothness" department. They rolled about as well as a bowling ball on the beach and gave off a sound that was reminiscent of a dental drill. But Richie D., on the other hand, had recently pulled off a small miracle and obtained the shiny, new Cadillac of inline skates: the fabled midnight black and royal purple Phantoms. *Phantoms!* Even the name itself was enough to take a man's breath away. They glistened in the sunlight like they were made from shiny black quartz and cast shadows on the skates of kids like me. They instantaneously catapulted Richie D. to a legendary status among the other skaters in the neighborhood. He was able to skate backwards with a new coolness, almost a Michael Jackson-like moonwalk that gave him enough suave and unearthly finesse that he became known by another name, one that still suits him to this day.

Rico.

Rico, Red, and I had agreed to meet at the Jr. High School that we all attended and it was just after noon that Saturday when we found ourselves skating around the run down, asphalt parking lot.

Rico skated backwards, his hair blowing softly in the wind, Pantene shine glistening in the sunlight, and I watched him until I felt slightly nauseous, and maybe even a little bit gay. And once I felt the surplus of saliva that precedes every colossal upchuck, I began to wish that his graceful moonwalk would end with a tiny pebble lodging itself in the wheel of those shiny new Phantoms.

Childhood was funny like that. You could love your best friend with all your heart, but the minute he got what you wanted, be it a girl, Super Mario Brothers 2, or that brilliant new pair of Phantoms, you could immediately wish an unrelenting barrage of bad things to happen to him.

I talked Rico into letting me try on the skates and minutes later I was carving through the blacktop jungle with animal-like agility. I flew across the paved beauty of Middle America's biggest city without a care in the world. I jumped and landed a perfect 180 and followed it up with a majestic 360. I was like Scott Hamilton, only much cooler and manlier.

I finished my session and minutes later the three of us were sitting on a parking block breathing heavily. I took off Rico's skates and began to reveal the details of my diabolical scheme.

I spoke slowly while Rico and Red listened with wide eyes that flickered in the late morning sun. I told them how I had discreetly unhinged the lock on the window to the boys locker room and how at that very moment, while we prepared to make history, all the treasures and fortunes associated with seventh grade lie waiting behind the cold, steel doors of the school.

When I felt sure that Rico and Red understood the plan, and I was comfortable in the fact that they wouldn't freeze up the minute we got inside, I made my way around the school where the window to the locker room was. Using the small water pipe affixed to the outside of the building, I shimmied up the wall, through the unlocked window, and onto the floor of the locker room. Once inside, I dashed through the locker room door, down the hall, and six calculated seconds later, I was letting Rico and Red into the building.

Upon entering, we paused and listened. It seemed that all of our senses had heightened and we had become intuitively aware of our surroundings. We slowly canvassed the scene with furrowed brows and shallow breaths, suddenly becoming aware of the fact that S.W.A.T. teams and A.T.F. helicopters could appear at any moment. We searched for the telling red dots that indicated the presence of sniper rifles and once we were moderately assured that none of our heads were in immediate danger of being blown into small, bite sized pieces, we entered into the gym.

The Gym. Two words, six letters, that when put together spelled nirvana. The gym smelled of sweaty clothes and burnt popcorn, and it buzzed from the sound made by the radiators that hung on the walls. It gave off a competitive vibe that made one instinctively reach for a red, rubber ball to throw or a giant parachute to toss. It had a shiny, freshly waxed, tiled floor that sparkled like diamonds reflecting prisms of sunlight. It held six basketball hoops, a wooden stage on which we would later perform a number of shamelessly boring plays, a kitchen in which to cook pancakes for the biannual pancake breakfast, a climbing rope that hung from the ceiling (the arch nemesis of every pudgy seventh grader), a small army of dented folding chairs and tables, and a balcony that was used mostly for storage.

To the casual observer it was just a normal gym for normal kids in normal junior high school. But we knew better. We knew the truth. Hidden on the balcony, just out of the eyesight of John Q. Public was the key, the answer, the crucial ingredient to the afternoon's fun: the legendary Port O' Pit.

The Port O' Pit was a crash mat so big and soft and green that it could catch falling skydivers and even the occasional asteroid. It was three feet of thick foam that promised to fend off broken bones and cracked skulls so long as you didn't completely miss it when you landed.

With me leading the way, the three of us climbed the ladder to the top of the balcony. Just as we suspected, the Port O' Pit was stashed in the corner, and after a number of heaves and hos, we were able to toss the Port O' Pit off of the balcony and onto the ground.

Once it was positioned properly on the gymnasium floor we started jumping, flailing, tripping, laughing and yelling until, right as we were all on the top of the balcony performing pre flight inspections on each other, the unbelievable happened. Someone entered the school! Our hearts stopped beating and time slowed. The three of us fell to our stomachs as quickly as we could, but we sensed that the jig was up! Our lives as free citizens of America were over. We were busted! Home cooked meals and waterbeds were going to be replaced by "three hots and a cot." I was going to be renamed Sally or Betsy, and we were all going to become somebody's bitch!

The three of us lay as flat as we could atop the balcony. We heard the gym door open and someone entered. Fear caused our body temperatures to rise and our Hypercolor shirts began to change from hot pink to forest green, the same color as the balcony floor. Amazingly, we were almost camouflaged. No one made a sound. No one breathed. I think Rico may have farted a little, but that was it. We were stealth ninjas, chameleons, the masters of our own destiny. Not even Scott the Janitor, who would later make a run at the world record for longest stay in the Chicago Christian School System, could catch us.

We waited until we were sure that whoever had entered the gym had left and hastily made our way out of the school. We had danced with danger and it pulsated through our blood. We were pioneers of peril. We had risked everything for the sake of a good time and we were alive with the vitality of our youth.

We exchanged excited looks and congratulated one another on jobs well done. But it was getting to be late afternoon and Rico and Red needed to get going. We said our goodbyes and I watched them skate away across the black asphalt. My friendship with Rico was stronger now and we could both sense it. In a way, we had been in battle together and both of us came out alive. We had pushed the envelope and skirted the confines of our adolescence because we yearned to feel the tingle of rebellion. It validated us, made us feel unstoppable.

While Rico and Red felt that pushing their luck and trying the stunt again was a bad idea, I ended up breaking into that school a few more times. I never came out with much, a few dollars stashed in a teacher's desk or a couple cans of pop, but I always felt guilty about what I took. I guess it was really never about the loot, but the rush I got by pushing the limits and doing something I knew I shouldn't have been doing.

As with most good things, this one came to an end as well. One of the neighbors saw me breaking in one day and called the police, who promptly arrested me. I spent a number of long hours in the holding cell of the police station that day, staring at the bars and waiting for my parents to cool off and come get me. They were mad, to say the least, but who could really blame them. I was awfully young to be getting picked up at the police station.

Being a kid was a tough racket and somehow, as an adult now, I can appreciate it a lot more. Perhaps Walt Disney said it best when he said, "Too many people grow up. That's the real trouble with the world, too many people grow up. They forget. They don't remember what it's like to be twelve years old. They patronize, they treat children as inferiors. Well I won't do that."

Neither will I.

The Fastest Kid

How did it get so late so soon?
It's night before its afternoon.
December is here before it's June.
My goodness how the time has flewn.
How did it get so late so soon?

Dr. Seuss

When the backdrop of your childhood is Chicago's notorious south side, there are certain things in life that just are. Take baseball for instance. It's conceivable that you could grow up watching America's favorite pastime and at one point in your life proclaim your undying devotion to the New York Yankees. Well, if you grew up on the south side of Chicago and tried to pull that shit, I'm pretty sure a gang of overweight, high-top and gym short wearing Sox fans would walk right out of Comisky Park (real Southsiders still call it that) to deliver you a big bag full of ass whoopin'. South side equaled Sox fan. And that was that.

Early on in life, baseball loyalty could ignite fistfights. Messing with the home team was an infraction that just would not be tolerated. I remember little Freddie Spitzer was sent home from third grade once for rubbing poor Bobby Meeker's face in an anthill when he admitted he was a Cubs fan. Sometimes, it got ugly.

Back then, though, life really did seem simpler. Baseball was pure and gave us an identity in a time when we were still searching for one of our own. It gave us something to root for and fight for and get dirty for. Comisky Park was our Canaan; a promised land filled not with milk and honey, but caramel corn and peanuts and hot dogs the size of Volkswagen Beetles. It taught us competition and gave us drive. It taught us life lessons we would later take with us as we journeyed into adolescence, and finally, adulthood. But perhaps most importantly, it taught us that everything in life was a race for something. And that something, as fate would have it, could turn into a lifelong friendship.

When a young man travels through the grade school ranks he begins to realize that schools, while priding themselves as being purveyors of equality and justice, actually operate through an ever present hierarchy. You can be a geek or a jock or a shoe in for the class clown, but perhaps no position in all of grade school commands as much respect and reverence as that of the Fastest Kid.

Holding the title of Fastest Kid is prestigious to children in the way the President is prestigious to politicians. It's a Michael Jordan-like title that allows you V.I.P. access to the most coveted of kid treasures. Good lunch trades, number one pick in the dodge ball draft, and sure fire notification of any dirty magazine sightings were all luxuries one could enjoy while wearing the Fastest Kid crown. And since life at that particular point in childhood revolved around races, anything and everything could be settled with a little friendly competition. Whether you were fighting with your best friend about kissing the same girl in the tunnel of love, or the nerdy kid in the front row had a green fruit roll-up with cutouts that you just had to have, the be-all end-all to settle the issue was a foot race.

It was the beginning of second grade when a little boy named Daniel made his way across the Canadian border and settled with his family just outside Chicago. He was tall and lanky, an anomaly amongst kids that age, and blessed with a mop of hair on his head that could have furnished wigs for both Mr. Clean and Daddy Warbucks. He spoke with an accent that was foreign to most of us at school and had a way of incorporating the word "*aye*" into almost everything he said. He hailed from the far away land of British Columbia, a place rumored to use a currency that resembled Monopoly money, and that conjured images in my head of muskets and red coats. I remember thinking that there was something different about Dan, something in his eyes that had my bright blue Hanes briefs all wadded up under my Levis. Who was this strange Canadian and what did he want? What did *really* want?

In second grade I prided myself in being somewhat of an amateur detective. I had gotten in the habit of reading Hardy Boy mystery novels, and was quite certain I could solve the J.F.K. murder mystery if I was only given the chance, so I put my ear to the playground and it wasn't long before I uncovered a plan that was so dark and so devious it sent a shiver down my boney little spine. Word on the street was that Dan was going challenge me to a race and make a play to remove my crown as Fastest Kid.

It was almost unheard of! A tall, lanky boy from Canada whose fancy for the word "*aye*" had him speaking sentences composed almost entirely of questions, was going to challenge me, the Fastest Kid, to a race? Unbelievable! It was an outrage, a public dismissal of all things sacred and good in the world of children!

But even though the challenge from Dan seemed to break all the unwritten rules of the playground simultaneously, the gauntlet had indeed been thrown and backing down was out of the question. There was only one thing to do. Train.

So train I did. Like a Carl Lewis prodigy I ran from one side of the playground to the other with a quickness and finesse that had not been seen since the days of the Ricochet Rabbit cartoon. I ran with an Olympic form that I swear had Steve Prefontaine himself smiling down on me from heaven. I raced buses and cars and friendly dogs until sweat gleamed off of my prepubescent body like fresh wax on 1967 Mustang Fastback. And when I finally took off my shoes to rest, I was a lean and mean, well oiled racing phenomenon. What some would call…a cheetah.

When race day finally came there was an excitement in the air that could be seen with the naked eye. Kids of all shapes and sizes had gathered along both sides of the sidewalk we would be racing down like rednecks at a NASCAR event. American flags flew mightily, the stars and stripes giving their blessing upon that great American tradition with each flap in the hot, summer breeze. Students were seen wearing shirts with pictures of cheetahs emblazoned on the fronts as signs of their steadfast loyalty to me. The teachers were off in one corner placing bets with the notorious school bookie, a little weasel of a kid named Bernie Warhol, no relation to Andy.

Near the starting line, I began to stretch, arching my back in a way that showed the ripples in all three of my muscles. I jumped up and down, shaking my head from side to side like I'd seen the boxers do on TV. I scanned the crowd and when I saw the beautiful Natalie Davis, I lingered for just a second. She was the real prize, the Winnie Cooper of Chicago Southwest Christian School. I gave her a quick smile and it was time to race.

Dan had shown up while I was scanning the crowd and a glance to my left side revealed to me someone who could only be described as the original Napoleon Dynamite. He had what looked to be a knee sock wrapped around his forehead and a pair of purple running shorts that made me instantly uncomfortable.

We had elected Johnny Hefler responsible for dropping the flag to signal the start of the race, and right before Johnny was to give the signal, I gave Dan one last chance to bow out and save face for his country. He turned towards me with beady eyes that pierced right through me, and in a voice that was an octave lower than the rest of the kids my age said, "*aye.*"

Once again I couldn't tell if it was a statement or a question, but one thing was as certain as the day is long, the race was on. We lined up and got in our running positions, ready to pounce at the slightest indication of movement by Johnny Hefler. Johnny raised his hands and the tension of the audience could have been cut with a knife!

Crack!

The starter gun fired and I was off the line like a fat guy on pasta. My legs were defying the natural laws of physics in a brilliant display of athletic heroism. I was moving at the speed of light, dangerously close to reaching eighty-eight miles per hour and disappearing back to the year 1985. I was seconds from the sheer victory and it had never felt so good! But just as I saw victory lane only a stone's throw away, Dan, the tall and lanky Canadian, passed me in a whirlwind of superhuman speed. He had fire and smoke streaming from his nostrils and he was running as if he had drunk super unleaded gasoline for breakfast. He passed me faster than a California wildfire in the middle of summer and disappeared in the distance ahead of me. It was if he had uttered some ancient, magic word that caused him to turn into Flash Gordon, and before I could even begin to protest, my title was gone.

I was devastated.

Dan met me at the finish line to shake my hand. I warily took it. I had lost the race, but, incredibly, I had won a friend. Over two decades of friendship later, and the Fastest Kid still can't successfully explain why Canadians say "*aye*" so much, and I still can't beat him in a race. It's funny how things happen in life, how insignificant events that occur when one tries to navigate the stormy waters of childhood end up being monumental, all the while paving the way for the future.

It wasn't too long ago that I had the honor of standing up in Dan's wedding and watching him get married on top of a mountain in Southern California. Ironically, it was yet another race won by the

Fastest Kid. As I stood there next to him while he gave his vows to his beautiful wife, it dawned on me how blessed I am to have a friend like him. I've lost a lot of things in my life, but losing that race was, perhaps, one of the best things to ever happen to me. It's good to know that when life begins to fall apart, as it inevitably does, there are good friends to help pick up the pieces.

My Search for Animal Chin

"When fun is outlawed, only outlaws will have fun."

Brian Brannon

In the early nineties, I went through what I now know was some sort of identity crisis that stemmed from my inability to determine whether I was going to be a biker or a skateboarder. I was torn between two loves, caught in a jealous tug o' war between four wheels and two. And if I knew anything at that age, it was that it was culturally impossible to be both. There was just no such thing as a biking skateboarder or a skateboarding biker.

I grew up down the street from what was known in my neighborhood as Central Trails. It was the BMX Mecca of the Southside and it attracted kids all the way from far away suburbs like the one my best friend Rico lived in. It was a dirt and mud kingdom that operated within a strict paradigm known only by the kids that went there. It was completely and utterly, one hundred percent, adult free.

If life was a school, then Central trails was my favorite classroom. It was populated by mostly older kids and because of this it was the place that I saw a lot of firsts. Saturday afternoons were a Petri dish of heavy petting, weed smoking, firework lighting, and little kid bullying fun. It was as if Central Trails existed in a parallel universe not known to adults, and run by society's troubled youth.

I think back to Central Trails and come to the conclusion that the road to adolescence is laden with potholes, perhaps none bigger than that of peer acceptance. And since being the youngest person at a place like Central Trails can work against you like a bad case of acne, I learned rather quickly that the best way to stay away from becoming the neighborhood version of Screetch was to make the older kids like me. I also knew that if I had anything going for me, it was the fact that I was willing to sacrifice my overall well being, and risk severe bodily harm for the sake of that cause.

Central Trails was notorious for a number of reasons, but the one thing that had kids in bunk beds tossing and turning endlessly throughout the hot, summer Chicago nights was the legendary Jump of Death. It was a ginormous jump, a perfectly sculpted dirt monstrosity that was fabled to have claimed the life of Jimmy Doyle a few years back. It was rumored that if one were to approach the jump with enough speed that one just might launch oneself right smack into the middle of orbit.

As the summer days wore on, I would proceed to attempt the Jump of Death in what some might call an extremely dangerous and stupid way of gaining some street cred. With each successful attempt, I would gain a little more confidence and would try to hit the jump with more and more speed until one day, as a crowd of older, much cooler kids stood watching and taunting, I approached the jump at a speed that would have impressed Evel Knievel himself. I launched so high into the earth's atmosphere that when I finally came down, I hit the ground with such a tremendous force that I bounced back into the air! Seconds later I came back down hitting the ground, for the second time, with a loud *"HMPH!"* as the air was forced out of my lungs by my chest hitting my handlebars and breaking them clear off the frame. As I gasped for air, laughter erupted from the crowd of cruel onlookers, and as I wheeled my broken bike away, mumbling curse words under my breath, I decided a change was in order.

It wasn't long after that that I left bike riding behind for guys like Matt Hoffman and Lance Armstrong, and the bike with the broken handlebars found a permanent place in my parent's garage. I had decided it was time to make the foray into skateboarding, and like everything else I had done in life up to that point, I was jumping in feet first. It was skate or die. The Bones Brigade, the Tony Hawk haircut, Speed Cream, Sex Wax, the infamous movie *"The Search for Animal Chin,"* and the king of all cheap, yet somewhat envied, skateboards, the Executioner.

At the time, The Executioner was the largest, heaviest, most impractical skateboard ever made. But unfortunately, it was also one of the most coveted possessions in all of Childrendom. In keeping with the times, it came in all of the 1990's most popular colors, each of which happened to be neon. There was a Day Glow Green, a Hot Neon Pink, and the ever popular, "I ate too many vitamins and now my pee is bionic" yellow, the color that was, for reasons I cannot presently remember, my personal favorite.

When I had learned the basics of skateboarding on the Executioner and came to the realization that a skateboard that weighed as much as my old man's Datsun was never going to turn me into the skateboard icon I yearned to be, I finally graduated to a Rob Roskopp deck. I kicked and pushed and ollied my way through the neighborhood like any carefree, careless, knuckle-dragging skateboarder would, and was soon made privy to one of the cardinal rules of growing up.

Skaters and bikers don't get along.

It was like the Sox/Cubs rivalry that had plagued the city since turn of the century. There was no middle ground, you had to choose your allegiance. Sox or cubs. Bike or skateboard. Those wonderful trails where I had successfully set records at now became so dangerous to ride by that hockey goalie pads and anti-aircraft missile launchers became Christmas list toppers. My status as a skateboarder now precluded me from getting from one side of the neighborhood to the other without enduring mind numbing ridicule and mockery or setting new land speed records.

I spent a lot of that summer on the top bunk of my bed trying to figure out how I was going to remedy this growing problem. Two of my best buddies lived on the other side of Central Trails and I couldn't stop being friends with them because I was afraid an eighth grader was going to try and make me eat my skateboard for lunch. I figured that there were two ways I could successfully get past the bullies while still retaining my dignity. I could cross the street somewhere back by my house and ride past the trails from the opposite side of the street, or I could step up my game, swallow the lump in my throat, and haul my hairless little ass past the trails as fast as my bearings would allow.

On most occasions I would opt for the speed run, and since I was still bitter about my exile from the trails, I got in the habit of yelling certain taunting phrases while whizzing past. *"Bikers Suck!"* and various forms of the ever popular *"Your Mama!"* type jokes were some of my favorites. It became sort of a game for me, an entertaining way of getting my adrenaline going.

The reaction was always the same, too. My taunts would cause chaos to erupt as bikers would scramble to mount their BMX's and catch whoever dared try and defame the raunchy bunch. Snarling bikers would spill out onto the sidewalk, mouths foaming, as they made one ineffectual attempt after another to catch the fastest kid on four wheels. Even back then, I showed signs of being a ninja.

Summer carried on much like it does when you're a kid, and before long the threat of school cast a shadow onto the bustling neighborhood. I'd performed my little stunt quite a few times that summer, and as August wore on the bikers had figured out who I was. I wasn't a rocket scientist by any means, but one of the few things I did know was that if I ever had any intention of being a graduate of junior high school, I would need to lie low for a while until the heat died down.

I started crossing the street to go visit my friends, and although I still got mean looks and threatening stares from across the four lanes of traffic that separated me from them, it was mostly uneventful.

School started and Central Trails was barren during the week except for the occasional kid who faked a sick day. I no longer had to fear the Trails as I did in the summer. The slow moving classroom life had returned.

The summer of my Central Trails switch I watched the movie *"The Search for Animal Chin"* over and over. In it, the Bones Brigade traveled all over California in search of legendary skateboard master Animal Chin, who had gone underground, saying that skating had become too commercial.

I look back on that movie now, and I think that, somehow, maybe my childhood has gone underground; maybe adulthood has become too commercial. I miss Central Trails and everything it represented because it was childhood innocence at its greatest. I know now that life moves quickly, and if you don't take the time to make memories, you'll never have time to remember them.

The Channel One Conundrum

*"Since Channel One doesn't seem to work, it behooves parents
to ask that it be removed. It is their children who will have to pay the
price if they don't."*

The Houston Chronicle, May 18, 1994.

Back in the old days, or as every parent of the seventies seems to call them, the *good* old days, I was one of those kids that was constantly in trouble. I think my first, and possibly second, words were of the four letter variety and were immediately followed by the sound of my mother choking on her dinner. Still, to this day, my mother swears my first word was "duck," but there's a big part of me that begs to differ.

To put it simply, I was a handful. To put in my mother's terms, I was big pain in the ass. But it wasn't like I was really ever *trying* to get in trouble. It just seemed to me that most of the fun things in life were things I wasn't supposed to do. In fact, I got in so much trouble in junior high school that my friends and I had T-Shirts made up for our teachers when we finally graduated eighth grade bearing the truism "I survived the class of '92." It was a juvenile, yet somewhat effective attempt to reconcile with the enemy, to call a truce if you will. Maybe even a consolation prize to remind them who had eventually won the yearlong battle of wills. I suppose, in a sense, we figured that with high school inching closer and closer, we needed to tally are losses and start fresh with the administration.

So start fresh we did. The onset of high school brought about a whole new level of competition. And it was because of this reborn sense of relentless competition, that we found ourselves reaching deep down inside, where our inner children sat crouched in the corner pooping, in search of our A games. Everything had become a competition: girls, detentions, sports, pranks, and even academics to a certain extent, since we were willing to concede to the fact that were some courses you simply just had to pass.

It was during freshman year, in a move that left us scratching our heads in amazement, that the administration decided they were going to have televisions installed in every classroom. The move was in direct response to the overall consensus by adults that high school kids were out of touch with global news and what was going on around the world in general. The school was being unoriginal in almost every way by following the lead of some of the other local establishments and installing the televisions so that we could watch a syndicated news show geared towards kids that went by the amazingly unique and obviously well thought out name, Channel One.

The Channel One decision was big in the sense that electronic technology was still somewhat unheard of in our school. TV's weren't yet quite as popular as they are today and certainly weren't seen in automobile headrests and men's restrooms. It was still pretty common to see a thirty-two inch Zenith connected to a four head VCR being wheeled from class to class when it was time to watch epic documentaries like "*Egypt: The place with lots of sand.*"

Channel One was able to claw its way into school classrooms around the country by offering to loan TV equipment to the establishments in exchange for the promise to have its students watch the show. The show itself, a twelve minute news segment with a variety of special sections like the ever popular "Pop Quiz!" or "Question of the Day," featured news with a modern and pop cultural twist. It actually employed a few names, like Serena Altschul, that we would later see in mainstream media. (Think MTV.)

The whole concept of Channel One was simple enough: show news and commercials in exchange for TV's and VCR's. It was appealing to schools that lacked funding for such luxuries and in 1993, when I was a scrawny freshman in an even scrawnier school, Channel One was implemented.

It was a strange day when we students showed up to find that the corner of every classroom now held, in perfect view for all of academia to see, bright, shiny, brand new televisions. The hallways buzzed as kids tried to figure out what it all meant. Were we finally going to be rid of teachers in lieu of video teaching? Had the staff's budget been slashed so much that they could only employ one teacher who would now have to videotape his or her lectures to be distributed to all the classes? Had we finally won the argument with faculty that the movie version of a book was much better than the book itself?

We didn't have to wait long before our wise principal's voice could be heard on the P.A. system answering our questions. And it wasn't long after the principal's voice ceased to resonate from the speakers on the wall that the TV's became alive with music and the introduction to Channel One was seen. For twelve minutes we tried to figure out what exactly we were watching and why exactly we were watching it. But we didn't really care because we had all done the math in our heads and figured out that first period was now considerably shorter.

I sat in the back of the classroom that day and thought about how I could use this new television surplus to my advantage. There had to be some way that we could turn this Channel One conundrum into something completely and unreservedly entertaining.

The bell to end first period sounded and the class rapidly spilled into the crowded hall. I began scanning the faces of the students for one of my partners in crime and when my eyes landed on the toothy grin of Kyle Osterman, I knew he had already thought of the plan.

I met him by his locker and we walked down the hall towards our second period classes. As his eyes darted from side to side the way seedy villain characters in movies always do, he started to explain what he had concocted. And the minute he said those three magical words, I couldn't believe I hadn't thought of them myself. Universal remote control. I mean, looking back on it now from over a decade later, I'm appalled that the criminal calculator attached to the top of my neck failed to compute fast enough to claim sole credit for this diabolical plan.

But such is life and the next day, as promised, Osterman brought the universal remote control and it was game on. Algebra class, the high school equivalent to the torture method known as water boarding, was taught in a room that was connected to another room by a shared wall with a long window of tempered safety glass. The way the seats were positioned, Osterman could aim the remote control towards the TV in the room opposite ours while our teacher wasn't looking, hit the power button, hide the remote, and sit back and watch while the drama unfolded.

The other teacher, who was usually causing some poor, inept student to contemplate suicide by demanding the square root of 654 be calculated immediately, without warning, and in his head, would hear the television turn on and look around the room with a menacing glare that I'm pretty sure is exclusive to algebra teachers. Seeing no faces exuding any more fear than usual, he would calmly reach up and turn off the television, muttering curse words under his breath.

Back in our classroom, Osterman and I were shooting hysterical glances at one another trying to keep the snot from flying out of our nostrils. Thirty seconds later though, Osterman would do it again, which would cause the teacher in the other room to do the whole menacing glare thing again, and consequently, Osterman and I would again find ourselves withholding laughter with force that threatened to pop out our eyeballs.

For days this went on and for days we watched as the algebra teacher across the way slowly went crazy. At one point he actually implemented a search and seizure that would later be adopted by the TSA. It was fruitless, though, and as the days wore on he finally seemed to give in to this unexplainable poltergeist and began to teach with the television on.

Eventually, though, our prank was realized and the in-school suspension we endured gave us lots of time to think about our misgivings. But the more we thought about it, or at least the more I thought about it, the more I realized that we were only following the natural progression of life. We were students, jokesters, problem kids and it was our job to find ways to foil the teachers' plans and entertain our peers. We were the Road Runner and they were the Coyote and honestly, nobody ever really died from an ACME anvil.

From a Barnes and Noble bookstore that I hope to one day have a book in I reminisce about high school. I miss high school. Because a couple years after the Channel One conundrum, when I was kicked out of high school, I felt as if I was kicked out of childhood. I grew up so fast after that, that I didn't have time to watch the passing cars anymore. Because all of the sudden I was standing in the street.

Shakespearian Floosies

"Oh Romeo, Romeo, wherefore art thou, Romeo?"

Romeo & Juliet, Act II, Scene 2

The thing about the "glory days" is that we fail to recognize how much glory is actually in them until after they're gone. It's the whole 'the grass is always greener' syndrome, constantly yearning for a future where we're older and richer, and finally able to do all the things that we were forbidden from doing then. We're blind to the absolute magic of childhood until we're stuck at a desk in our late twenties trying to figure out where the hell recess and those last two abs went. The keg parties and girlfriend swapping that made high school the greatest time period in history since the era of Greek orgies, dissipated into thin air the moment we put away our favorite Converse All Stars in favor of the iconic penny loafer. It's an absolute tragedy.

But when I think about the "glory days" or the days that I somehow still manage to glorify at least once a day, it's almost impossible not to think about, of all things, Shakespeare.

I went to one of those high schools that other high schools made fun of. The entire institution was made up of no more than four-hundred people and all of the teachers were prehistorically Dutch and had secret recipes for oliebolin. Chances were, you sat in the same English class in the same English classroom and had the same English teacher as your mother. Consequently, this made your teacher roughly nine-hundred years old and able to speak dead languages fluently.

Naturally, with the majority of my teachers being able to recite Bible stories from firsthand experience, there was quite a bit of excitement lacking in our day to day activities. And by this I don't mean to discount the excitement of knowing someone that actually witnessed the parting of Red Sea, but when it came to being a teenager Moses couldn't hold a candle to Zach Morris.

You see, ever since I was able to maneuver my little diapered ass around the house, I have been searching for amusing ways to pass the time. Whether it was a carefully placed broomstick in the front wheel of my friend's bike as he rode past me or a hydrochloric acid bomb booby trap in the yard of the little old lady down the street, I always seemed to find a way spice up the monotony of my existence.

And I wasn't alone. As fate would have it, there were quite a few kids out there that grew up with the gene that made them root for the bad guy in movies. The kinds of kids that made pen guns and shot spitballs and actually pulled the infamous Flaming Bag of Poop trick.

The social circle I kept in high school extended a bit further, shall we say, than the narrow confines of my present mix of associates. There was a group of us, some might have even called us the popular ones (though I now think it wasn't so much popularity as it was sheer entertainment that kept us near the peak of the social pyramid), that all hung out and played soccer and smoked cigarettes and traded girlfriends and drank beers and spent a vast majority of our free time serving mind-numbing detentions. We liked the attention, the rush, the freedom we felt every time we disregarded the rules in favor of a classroom laugh or red faced teacher.

It was sophomore year on the South side of Chicago and my adolescent days were beginning to dwindle with each sounding homeroom bell. School was boring, interrupting my rigorous sleep patterns with homework assignments and exams. The spice in life had seemingly fled, leaving me craving havoc and mayhem and a certain senior girl.

It was a Tuesday morning and I had arrived to school early, a rare event since I spent as little time as possible there. And since the whole concept of life pre-homeroom bell was so brand new to me, I found myself aimlessly wandering the halls in search of nothing in particular. I walked and watched the flurry of kids slamming lockers and gossiping when it dawned on me that all the girls in my school had one painful thing in common: they all found it necessary to layer their clothing. It seemed that J Crew and Abercrombie & Fitch, the clothiers of choice for almost every female in my high school, had taken it upon themselves to advertise multi-layered dressing. It was totally unnecessary and posed a huge problem for anyone lucky enough to find themselves in the backseat of a cheerleader's car after a football game. Because now what was usually a leisurely walk from first base over to second involved fighting a sweatshirt, a flannel shirt, a t-shirt and a tank top all before you even saw a glimpse of bra strap. In fact, you almost had to start planning your make out sessions in advance based on the type of outfit you had to weed through. There was absolutely nothing quite as tragic and unforgiving as finding yourself halfway through the flannel jungle only to have your curfew stop you mid-grope.

Perturbed, but willing to accept it as a part of the adolescent experience, I continued my stroll down C hall until I saw Kyle Osterman rearranging books in his locker in order to close it. Kyle was one of those kids that had a locker that just never seemed to shut. He was constantly trying to do that maneuver where you push all the stuff inside with your hand as hard as you can, then pull it out while trying to slam the door shut. He wasn't very good at it though, and every time he tried to slam the door, one of his books would tumble out and wedge itself, making it impossible to close. It was really a rather comical thing to watch since this would go on for minutes on end. I always wondered why he just didn't clean his locker and put an end to the madness, but when he finally did manage to get the locker closed he would have this look of triumph on his face and new swagger in his step that told me he'd never change a thing.

Kyle was quite a bit shorter than I was and if it wasn't for the fact that he was one of the few sophomores that had actual, real, defined muscles under his shirt, I'm sure he would have been locked in a locker on more than one occasion. Not to mention the fact that he had five brothers and spent more time wrestling and fighting with his siblings than I had spent sleeping as an infant, and was about as tough as high school kids come.

I walked up to Kyle to and gave him the proverbial "wassup" and engaged in a conversation that I'm sure eventually came around to the topic of female anatomy. That was the thing about high school dialect, you could talk about anything at all and if you gave the conversation long enough, it would turn into something sexual. If you said something like, "Yo, I hate those new soccer balls we've been using," it was a sure bet there would be at least three Beavis and Butthead type responses. "Huh, huh, huh…balls!"

About halfway through our conversation, Kyle's beady eyes darted side to side and he reached into his backpack. When he withdrew his hand it was holding a VHS tape. But the look on Kyle's face told me it wasn't just any VHS tape, it was one of *those* VHS tapes, the kind that have horrible plots and vowel laden soundtracks. The kind where the industry's biggest stars had names like Ron Jeremy, Nina Hartley, and the infamous John Holmes.

My reaction was complete and utter disbelief. The hamster in my head was running as fast as it could and it became glaringly obvious to me as the pieces of the puzzle began to come together that I could make CCHS history. Moments and opportunities like this were like Halley's Comet sightings, you might get it once, but you probably wouldn't get it again. It was like the stars had aligned perfectly that day because my first period class was English, and this English class was being taught by one of those instructors that looked like he had never been young. Like he was born old. In fact, my mother had this very same teacher when she was at the school, and once when I asked her how old he was when he taught her she replied, "I don't know, old!"

In English class we were watching the movie version of Shakespeare's Romeo and Juliet. It wasn't enough that we had to painfully traverse our way through the "wherefore art thou's" of the printed version, but Old Man Meyer wanted us to witness, first hand, the Hollywood murdering of a literary masterpiece. I'm quite certain it was the second most boring movie I ever had the pleasure of watching, being trumped only by the infamous Charlton Heston in the epic film *"The Ten Commandments."*

What this all meant was that just mere steps away from the spot that I stood at that very moment was a fully functional, Sharp 4 Head Hi Fi Stereo VCR with its trademarked super picture. And attached to that beautiful, majestic piece of electronic wonderment was an equally amazing thirty-six inch Zenith television. It was as if the forces of mischief had gotten together and decided to give me an early birthday present. I was caught in a tractor beam of deliberate and unconcealed tomfoolery!

I gave Kyle what kids all over the United States education system know as "the look," and asked him for the tape. He obliged and seconds later I was embarking on a mission so stealthy and ninja-like it's amazing I'm not a Navy S.E.A.L. today.

I entered the empty, unattended room with my heart pounding against my rib cage like a xylophone. I carefully ejected the misguided children of both the Capulets and the Montegues and inserted what I just knew was going to be revered as an instant classic.

I retraced my steps back into the hallway and disappeared into the crowd. School was about to begin and while I was busy setting up my sinister prank, the hallways had filled. I counted down the minutes until the bell rang and the weight of what I had just done began to sink in. As kids walked past me making their way to their classrooms I started to think that maybe this wasn't such a good idea after all. I mean, if I got caught, what was my punishment going to be? I couldn't quite remember reading the repercussions for porno swapping in the school's disciplinary handbook, but I had a sneaky suspicion that if I got caught, I was going to be punished in a way that the scholastic authorities had yet to think of.

The bell that signaled the beginning of first period rang and one by one, the crowds of students dispersed and began to file into their respective classrooms. I walked slowly towards first period, perspiration beginning to build under my arms, until I made it to the door. There was no going back now. I was pot committed, knee deep in a bowl of liquid shit.

I walked into the classroom and took my seat. I was three desks back from the television with a panoramic view of the madness that was about to unfold. The second bell, the one that signaled the start of class, rang and Old Man Meyer strolled to the front of the room. He greeted the class with his usual "good morning" and asked the class to bow their heads to open with prayer. This couldn't be happening! I had forgotten about the prayer! Now, not only was I facing some new form of cruel and unusual punishment by the administration, I was quite possibly going to hell for all of eternity. I would have to withstand fire and brimstone and eternal sunburn all in the name of comical entertainment. Inside my head my conscience was screaming *"Abort! Abort!"* but there was no aborting, no aborting whatsoever.

When the prayer ended I was quite sure that a bolt of lightning was going to shoot from the sky and strike me down. Old Man Meyer reached for the play button and time slowed like a scene from *The Matrix*. His finger touched the control and he began to walk towards the back of the class. There was a slight delay as I could hear the VCR begin to ready the tape for playback and as Meyer reached the back of the classroom, the dimly lit room filled up with flesh colored light. There in front of all to see were three women engaged in an act that no one in that room could ever have dreamed to be involved in. The volume of the television was turned to an obnoxiously loud level and a symphony of sexual sounds were echoing off the vanilla walls. The classroom gave a collective gasp and promptly erupted into a frenzy of laughter and wide eyed cackling. And from the look on the face of Ben

Weimar, one could only come to the conclusion that right there, in that English classroom on that fateful Tuesday morning; he had his very first sexual experience. It was sheer chaos!

When the daunting reality of what was actually happening in his classroom finally registered in his brain, a mind blowing sixteen seconds of smut had been broadcast to the students of CCHS. He raced to the front of the class and frantically pushed the stop button until the glow of sexual perversion fell black. There was nothing for him to do but stand there, stunned and suffering what looked to be some sort of agonizing bowel function.

The old man scanned the ruffled feathers of his favorite class and settled his accusing glare on the very spot where I was sitting. It was as if he knew that I was involved somehow, like I was the only student that could pull something like this off. He stared at me for a minute, silent, not saying anything. Our eyes locked. He was the teacher, I was the prankster. But he couldn't prove it and I knew it.

He finally spoke and said, "Hillegonds, was this you?"

And I responded with the only natural thing to say. "Nah, Mr. Meyer, I'm pretty sure that was Nina Hartley."

Old School

"I know God will not give me anything I can't handle.
I just wish He didn't trust me so much."

Mother Teresa of Calcutta

I once heard it said that if you didn't know where you'd been, you'd never get where you were going. To remind myself of this, every now and again I look back in time and reread words that I've written. I've filled countless pages with words that I've written to myself and, sometimes, to God, words that I'd written years ago to try and purge myself from a lifetime of guilt.

I wrote this not too long after I had moved back from Colorado, a feeble attempt at trying to reconcile all that had happened while I was out there.

It had been a while since I sat down and really thought about God and what I had to say to Him. We'd had this on-again off-again relationship for the greater part of my teen and post teen years, but lately He had been getting my attention by more or less slapping me across the face. He'd been reprioritizing my life through the drama that had been unfolding the previous five years. In not so many words, He'd forced me to put my life into perspective. Through tragedy He'd shown me exactly how unimportant the things that at times seemed imperative really were. But the lessons I'd learned had been hard and I found myself wishing that I could feel Him more. I was scared I guess, scared of having to sleep in the bed that I'd made.

There was a nine month period of my life that seemed endless. Constant turmoil, excessive bickering, court dates, job interviews, fights, handcuffs, jail cells, bottles, blunts, and pills all played part in the day by day longing for some sort of personal freedom. I wanted closure for everything I had ever done and said and I wanted it now. I wanted the pain that I felt to stop, or at least subside, and I was willing to give up all my tomorrows to make it sting a little less. I had lost sight of all my dreams. All the hopes and aspiration that I had when I was a little boy were replaced with the chaos that surrounds one when one tries to run away from pain.

I remember gasping for air, fighting for oxygen while the world strengthened its chokehold around my neck. I remember reaching for God but feeling nothing, desperately searching for a handhold that just didn't seem to be there.

And that was when it happened.

God rocked my world in a way that I never saw coming. It was a divine backhanded slap to the face, the first real backhand I'd ever felt from Him. It wasn't a love tap; rather, it was one of those knock-the-sense-back-into-you slaps that fathers give their sons when they really screwed up. My girlfriend was in labor and everything in the entire universe stopped. The world didn't spin and the ocean's waves didn't break and all I could do was shake with the fear that I would be a horrible, horrible father. I didn't know what I was feeling. All I knew was that I was a nineteen year old kid who was about to have a baby and the thought of screwing up was paralyzing. I had money to make, bills to pay, sorries to say, and a million other places to be. I wanted to run. Again. Or drink or snort lines or eat pills, but the second my girlfriends murderous screams towards the hospital staff gave way to the muffled cry of innocence taking its first gulp of recycled air, something happened. At that point in time, in that split second, I felt what I had never in my entire life felt before. Complete serenity. In that moment nothing mattered, nothing but being there and feeling what I was feeling. Life was laid out before my eyes in the form of a magnificent little girl and for the first time I was able to put all of my life into its proper place.

Years later I look back on that day and I wonder if I'm still just as scared as I was back then. I still struggle to be a father and I miss Haley with every breath that I take. Our relationship is strained, tormented even, and I sometimes wonder if it will ever be better. I am stronger now though. Without vodka to cloud my vision I can see things more clearly. So I continue to put one foot in front of the other trying to get where I'm going. I continue to live life, even when it's hard, stopping every once in a while to see where I've been.

The T- Shirt Pillow

"There's no place like home. There's no place like home."

Dorothy, The Wizard of Oz

The door to the apartment I had shared with my girlfriend slammed behind me and Old Man Winter laughed. I had nowhere to go. I was homeless.

When that realization hit me, that I was homeless, I got one of those surreal feelings that come when something happens to you that you just never dreamed could ever be possible. And I don't know why, but of all the things that should have been going through my head right then, like where I would live or who I could call, I was remembering back to the day that I lost my first tooth. I was six years old and I had wiggled it with my tongue incessantly until a faint but steady stream of blood flowed to the back of my mouth and finally, with the help of my grabby little fingers, the tooth had come out. I beamed with pride and held the tooth up like a trophy for my mother to see. I was ecstatic, euphoric almost, that I had finally crossed the threshold from little kids into the land of big boys. My mother told me to put it under my pillow that night, and if I went to sleep like a good boy, the Tooth Fairy would come and take my tooth, leaving me with a surprise in its place.

That evening, as the dark of night fell onto our little house on Central Avenue, I carefully place my prized tooth under my pillow. My heart beat faster than normal as I anticipated the next morning. I couldn't believe that the Tooth Fairy was actually coming to see me. After all, I was just a kid. An average kid in an average town and it was just an average tooth.

I pondered all of those things while staring at the glow in the dark stars my mom and I had pasted on the ceiling and it wasn't long before I was fast asleep. When I woke the next morning, I looked under my pillow and just like my mother had promised, the Tooth Fairy had come! She had left me two of the shiniest quarters I had ever seen in my entire life. I picked them up and held them. I studied them closely, looking for signs of magic dust or Tooth Fairy markings or anything to distinguish them from regular quarters. I smelled them. They were only two quarters, but to me they were proof; proof that magic existed and even average little kids like me could find it.

The cold air picked up a bit and I snapped out of my memory, adjusting the big duffle bag on my shoulder. I needed that magic now more than ever. I needed that magic to stop the constant bickering with my girlfriend, which always led to fighting, which always led to yelling, which always led to the neighbors calling the police, which always led to me wearing those despised silver bracelets. I needed that childhood magic because I was burnt out on life. I was tired. I was on a first name basis with most of the officers in the local police department and I was dangerously close to becoming a criminal statistic.

But it was a catch twenty-two.

Because when I chose to leave my girlfriend, when I decided that leaving her was the only way for me to ever be anything, or do anything, I left to nothing. I tried to pack my clothes but she immediately unpacked them. She had bought them she said. I didn't deserve them she said. I was a loser she said.

It was difficult, but I was able to eventually put a few things into a big, red duffle bag. Ironically, it was the same big, red duffle bag that I that I had moved out there with just three short years earlier. I had my entire net worth in my pocket: sixty dollars. I had no friends around. I had no car. And now, I had no home. I was leaving my daughter and her sister. I was leaving the two most important things in my life and I fucking hated myself for it.

I walked out the door that day to a world of uncertainty. It was the one of those moments in life that was completely and utterly unmapped. I had no plan. I had no inclination whatsoever what I was going to do. But, ironically, walking out that door, closing it, and making a decision to change, or at least try to change, felt good.

At least for a second.

Because after that second was over the reality of what I had done hit me like brass knuckles to the teeth. It hit me like a runaway truck. Reality hit me with a left hook to the body that caused me to double over and gasp for breath on the side of the road.

I walked to the nearest bar, went inside, sat down on an uncomfortable barstool and spent the only money I had on the one thing that could anesthetize my pain.

Vodka.

I ordered a drink, took a sip, and in the split second that followed I understood why I drank. I drank because for a few hours while I refilled those clear glasses with that clear liquor, for a few cherished hours, I could escape from the haunted house of reality that had become my life. When I drank I aspired. I thought of how I would get myself out of my predicament, how I would prevail, how I would take a deck stacked against me and throw down a royal flush. When I drank I dreamed. I dreamed of being a good dad and great husband and a successful business man. Everything was possible from that barstool, but the minute I left it my dreams faded away.

I drank until the money was gone and left the bar. I started walking down the street, the mountains towering over me, everything I owned in life at the time packed in a beat up duffle bag thrown over my shoulder. I walked through the blistering cold of a clear Colorado night. I walked a mile in the kind of cold that chilled bone marrow. I walked until my face was numb and my fingers hurt and eventually, I arrived at a Denny's restaurant.

It was late and the graveyard server was handing out Grand-slam breakfasts to what was left of the bar rush. I walked through the double doors of the restaurant, nodded at the server, and made my way to the booths in the back. The booths were empty and the lights were dimmed. I picked out the largest booth, the six top in the corner, took a t-shirt out of my bag and made a makeshift pillow. I laid down, closed my eyes, and settled in to what would be my bed for many nights to come.

Scars

"When I stand before thee at the day's end, thou shalt see my scars and know that I had my wounds and also my healing."

Rabindranath Tagore

"**G**et up."

The flashlight beam force fed accusing rays of light into my retina and I woke from one bad dream into another. The vodka or beer or gin or whatever else I had been drinking earlier still had a firm grasp on my sense of reason, but the ever present cackle of the police radio told me my night wasn't getting any better. I sat up, then stood, and heard the phrase that I lovingly referred to as my mantra.

"Put your hands behind your back."

If I could pick six words in the English language that I hated the most, these would be them. By this point in my sorry, rebellious, angry, lonely, I-don't-give-a-fuck existence, I had managed to hear these six words so many times that they sounded normal. It was business as usual.

I was standing in the apartment that I had shared with Haley's mother the greater part of the last two years and as the handcuffs tightened around my wrists, I started to piece together the night.

"You gonna tell us what happened?"

They always asked that. It was the cop way of trying to get you to say things to implicate yourself. They always said it in a way that led you to believe that by explaining your actions or apologizing for what you'd done, you could somehow be exonerated or freed with a stern scolding. The reality was, though, that your best bet in any situation involving Johnny Law was to stay as tight lipped as you possibly could, and call your lawyer the minute you got the chance. If you were already in handcuffs, the cops had enough probable cause to arrest you. Until a judge said otherwise, you were heading to the clink.

Outside the apartment, winter raged in the state that I now called home and the ever laborious task of trying to make things work with Haley's mom had gotten to the point where I was couch surfing at a friend's house. Meaning things weren't working. At all. Haley's mom and I couldn't get through a conversation without wanting to kill one another and the two small kids, one of which bore a striking resemblance to me, had unfortunately become leverage.

We had been apart for a few weeks and I had fallen into a daily routine that consisted mostly of beer and work. I had a respectable job working as a "grunt" for the power company and spent most weekdays four wheeling through the mountains and taking home a pretty good sized paycheck. I worked and drank and ate and slept and drank and worked and did everything I could not to dwell on the latest pitfall of a relationship that spent more time on the verge of disaster than a Hollywood romance.

Earlier that evening, Baby Mama had called and begged that we get together to talk. But it was only after I was well into my tenth beer that I obliged. Another horrible choice in a growing list of horrible choices.

"What happened to the door?" the cop asked.

I looked in the direction of the door as the cop began to lead me towards it and became painfully aware of the fact that this door was never going to shut properly again. There were splinters of wood littering the carpet around the base of the doorway and where the deadbolt housing used to be, was now a crack running the length of the doorjamb.

It had obviously been kicked in, probably by me, but I told the cop I had no idea what had happened and walked out of the broken doorway and into the freezing mountain air. The alcohol on my breath came out in opaque clouds. My thinking was foggy. The cop guided me down the three stairs that led up to the place that I once called home. Seconds later, the door to the police car slammed shut behind me and the familiar smell of lost freedom filled my nostrils.

I gazed out the window of the police car as the reality of what was going on started to dawn on me. Another night was ending with me in the back of a black and white dancing to the pulsating rhythm of the reds and blues. My eyes stung and my brain pounded. My mouth was dry and I wanted to smoke. I clenched my eyes closed and forced myself to think.

It came back to me in fireworks of clarity, bright explosions of memory that lit up my mind with bits and pieces of information from the last few hours. I remembered a car ride, tears, talking, yelling, screaming and hurting from being two people, too young, with too many problems. I was a nineteen year old father trying to make it work with a twenty year old mother and I was failing dejectedly. I was angry and scared and immature. I was a grade A fuck up who was kicked out of high school and a shoe in for the inmate license plate program. I was a criminal in the back of a police car trying to figure out what the fuck had happened.

I opened my eyes but my reality hadn't changed. I was still in handcuffs that were digging into my wrists and in front of the car in which I was held captive; the officers were talking and glancing in my direction with quick, condemning stares.

I thought back.

I had been sitting in a friends run down, two bedroom apartment on the couch that I had been using as my bed for the last few weeks when Baby Mama had called and insisted that we talk. She didn't want to be apart any longer and wanted to reconcile and try to salvage whatever it was she thought we had had. I hesitated, knowing that the ten beers I had already ingested would lessen the blows of having to rehash the hell of a relationship we had been living in for the last year, but also knowing the alcohol would lubricate my tongue.

I loved Baby Mama for a time, at least I think I did, but it was the unhealthy sort of love that is born of rash decision and rebellion. It was painful love bred from uncertainty and insecurity and it took every ounce of strength my seditious soul could muster.

The cop got into the police cruiser and did his best to ignore me and we pulled away, leaving behind the little bit of familiarity I had. The mountains slowly moved in the background, looming ominously over a valley that I could never call home. I missed my city and my fast paced life back in Chicago. I missed Fastest Kid and Rico every second of every minute that I had been out there, and wished that I was back with them at that very moment. I wanted to be in college with them, doing keg-stands and beer bongs in between classes. I wanted to be dating new girls from new cities and wowing them with stories of being a professional in-line skater. I wanted to be cruising around with Rico on Friday night in his Blazer bumping Bone Thugs until we set off car alarms. I wanted my old life back.

The police cruiser sped up and only minutes later, we had pulled up to the police station. The cop in the front seat got out and opened my door, instructing me where to go. Slowly, deliberately, we climbed up a few steps and into a room with bright white lights and an industrial paint job.

"Have a seat." barked the cop.

I sat down and heard the clink of metal on metal as I was handcuffed to the table. I looked around the room, blinking rapidly, trying to ward off the annoying radiance that was invading my dry eyes. The room was small and cold and built only for two things: fear and admission. I could sense the cops watching me as I looked over at the one way glass, wondering how much trouble I was really in.

I put my head down and stared into the table, once again forcing myself to think, piecing together the night.

Baby Mama had shown up at the apartment that I had been staying in and insisted that we go for a ride. She wanted to get me away from the beer, away from my friends, away from anything that would distract me from her. She wanted to drive and talk, to try and navigate our maze of a relationship while winding through icy mountain roads. She wanted me to hear her side of the story. But the facts were this: I had co-written the story with her and I already knew it. I didn't want to hear it again. I didn't want to hear anything from her except the sound her footsteps made as she walked away. I was a fucking failure in every sense of the word and being with Baby Mama only made me less likely to ever change. She wanted me to fulfill the roll of father/provider when I couldn't rub two fucking nickels together. She wanted me to be thirty and mature when I was having a hell of a time being twenty and immature. I didn't know the answer to the million dollar question that would set us free, but I had sure as hell used up my 50/50 and ruled out a future with her as my final answer.

I got in her car and she began to drive. We drove northwest, steering the car deeper into the mountains and further away from everywhere I wanted to be. The silence in the car was so loud it was deafening. The roads, like Baby Mama's stares, were icy and cold and the warm embrace of alcohol that had been holding me had begun to let go. It was just her and I and a world of problems. Two kids with mounting anger that mistook codependency for love. Two kids with two kids who knew way too much about responsibility and the ramifications of irresponsibility. Two angry, fucked up kids with no one to blame except for the person sitting next to them, and a mounting rage confined to the inside of a car.

The talking started.

Small talk took a backseat to big issues. We drove and talked and yelled and screamed and hurt and cried and tried to work out our problems with algorithms that were all wrong. We came up with no answers and no solutions and there wasn't a cuss word that had ever been said that could project how I felt. I hated her with the same ferocity that I loved her with and the feeling was mutual. We couldn't make it together and we were proving that we couldn't make it apart.

My body was rigid and my teeth clenched as I forced out sentences that did more harm than good. I let the alcohol tear down whatever ounce of self control I had left and I screamed at her to leave me alone and to let me out of the car. I wanted to know why she was doing this and what she wanted from me. I just wanted out. Out of the car and out of her life and out of this God forgotten place with its condescending fucking mountains.

I begged her to turn the car around and take me back but she was in command and she was calling the shots. She controlled the gas pedal to the car and set the speed limit for our conversation, which had veered almost completely out of control. Reason and logic had left a long time ago and all that was left were crocodile tears and *fuck you.*

I unloaded staccato, machine gun screams at her that came from deep within, purging my wounded soul as they brought anarchy to the remaining calm. I commanded her to stop the car, to let me out, to let me run the fuck away from her and this responsibility, but it was no use and the closest thing to stopping she came to was thirty-five miles per hour.

My veins pumped diesel fuel and I felt hatred and fury take over. No more. No more. No more motherfucking games. No more pain and hurt and jealousy and anger. No more tears and sick love. No more crystal meth. No more talking and trying and failing and losing. No more hedonistic resolve. No more me. No more me.

At thirty five miles per hour I opened the door and got out. My right foot hit the ground as Baby Mama let out a scream I couldn't hear. My work boot hit the road and dust kicked up while I gave it my weight and brought out my left foot. I let go of the door and for a split second, I teetered the line between life and death.

I saw things in slow motion.

The cold wind hit me with brute force so strong it threatened to knock me over as the car inched in front of me. I somehow kept my balance, though, skidding forward to the screech of rubber until the soles of my work boots finally caught, catapulting me from slow motion to fast forward. I was airborne for a split second before hitting the ground running and sprinting out the rest of the distance it took me to slow down.

Baby Mama kept driving as I stood in the middle of the deserted street cursing everything I knew. My breath came out like dragon's fire and every muscle in my body was pulsing with adrenaline. I was out of my fucking mind and I wanted to fight. I wanted to hurt and maim and kill and fuck up and tear down and break. I wanted to punch someone or something. I wanted to feel my fist break bone and scar something beautiful.

I wanted to scar something beautiful.

I was two blocks from the place where Baby Mama and I used to live together and in the distance I could see the car that I had just exited turn the corner. I broke into a sprint that could have set Olympic records. I streaked down the street and around the corner, eyeing Baby Mama's car in the distance as I drew closer to it.

"IS THIS WHAT YOU WANT?! IS THIS WHAT YOU FUCKING WANTED!! FUCK YOU! I FUCKING HATE YOU!!"

The wells to my eyes opened up while hate and love had become the same thing. Tears began to stream down my face in streaks of wet lightning as I ran and yelled. I got closer and saw the fear register on Baby Mama's face and I digested it. I thrived on it. I got to the door and told her to open it, but she was still in the car, and not moving fast enough.

"OPEN THE MOTHERFUCKIN' DOOR!"

I heard the words come out of my mouth, but I didn't know the person saying them. The Tim of years ago that loved things with innocent passion had long since vanished and all that was left was this angry, unstable shell. An exoskeleton that protected nothing because even though I could feel my heart beating, I knew it was dead.

Baby Mama was struggling to get out of the car, her eyes darting back and forth as if looking for help. She knew we were past the point of no return and the stakes of the game had been raised considerably. I was dangerous. I was out of control. I was in the midst of an alcohol and adrenaline fueled rage and there was no calming me down.

I turned to the door and exploded. All of my rage and fury concentrated into one kick and the door splintered into pieces. Wood and paint chips flew through the air like candy from a piñata and littered the carpet around the door. The once happy home now stood open and broken, just like I was.

I walked through the door, muscles tensed and hands balled into fists, my breathing hissing out of my clenched teeth. I tried to calm down. I tried to breathe, to force the adrenaline to subside, but I was a rabid pit bull off his leash and I would not heel.

My eyes scanned the room as I huffed and puffed, determined to blow the motherfucking roof off. Odium and detestation were the only things I felt and as I heard footsteps behind me, I turned to see Baby Mama walking in.

She glared at me with haunting, hateful eyes and I glared right the fuck back. All the love we ever shared was gone, replaced with a sick competitiveness for making rash, emotion induced decisions. I threw myself onto the couch like a child and buried my face in the couch cushions and screamed into a pillow. I knew I should leave. I knew I should go before the fight escalated any further, but I didn't. I wanted it. I wanted to hurt her as much as she hurt me. I wanted her to feel as much pain as I did, to feel as crazy as I felt.

I ripped my head from the pillow just enough to tell her I fucking hated her.

Her head whipped towards me and she jumped on my back with a flurry of fists raining down on me. Tears began to stream down her face as she yelled things about having my child and hating me just as much and how the fuck could I do this to her.

I absorbed the blows, feeling her fist bruise my back and shoulders and the back of my head. I grew angrier with each punch and finally, with a snap of my neck, I whipped my head back and heard the satisfying crack of my skull connecting with her nose. She screamed and rolled off of me, holding her nose and crying as I stood up, manic with adrenaline.

She whimpered into her open palms and I reveled in it. It felt so good to hit her. To give her pain. To see her suffer. But even in the midst of all the craziness I knew it wasn't normal. That I wasn't normal. That I wasn't acting like a normal, rational human being. I didn't know who I was anymore. I didn't even know where I was. I didn't do this to people. I didn't have fights like this. I was just a kid and kids aren't supposed to have fights that end up with bloody noses and noise ordinance violations. This wasn't happening to me.

But it was.

A few minutes passed and the welcomed silence turned down the intensity. I stared at her, feeling less like a man that I ever had in my whole life, and she looked at me with hurt and sadness and pain. We just couldn't do it. We had tried so hard but everything we tried went wrong. We tried to love and ended up hating. We tried to act grown up and ended up losing our youth. We tried to carry the weight of our problems alone and ended up tired and beaten and lonely. We were the mess left after a tornado came through a town of glass houses—nothing left but shards of broken glass.

"You mind if we talk?" came the intrusive yet kind voice.

I was so lost in my memory that I almost forgot where I was. I lifted my head from the table and saw the familiar blue uniform of law enforcement, only this time it was draped over the body of a female officer. She stood in the doorway of the room that I was in with a notebook and waited for my answer. I shook my head up and down unhurriedly. She sat down next to me at the steel table. She advised me of my rights one more time and asked me if I wanted to explain to her what happened.

I told her I did.

I had false hopes. Unrealistic hopes. I thought that maybe I could somehow make everything better by owning up to what had just happened. I thought I would be doing the right thing if I just confessed to being in the wrong relationship with the wrong girl at the wrong part of my life.

I looked away from the officer and, once again, concentrated on the vanilla walls while I thought back to where things had gone wrong.

I stood towering over Baby Mama and she forced her tears to stop. She stood from the ground and walked into the kitchen. I knew that this fight had crossed the line. I knew that this fight had passed the breaking point, and there was no amicable ending in sight. I felt like I was holding a grenade with the pin pulled and I just couldn't find the strength to throw it.

She walked into the kitchen to get away and I followed her, prodding her with snide comments. I said things that would end up in Eminem songs years later. I hurled verbal atomic bombs. I spit manure from my potty mouth until she turned around in a crazed display of hatred and began to punch and hit and push. She was wildly swinging while I screamed obscenities back at her with unbelievable ferocity.

She screamed, I cried, she hit, I yelled, and in the blink of an eye, I hit her with a right cross in the arm with so much force that it broke it. She cried out in pain, the culmination of hurt and astonishment taking the form of a long and drawn out vowel. She looked at me, glared at me, hated me with all the strength she could muster.

I saw the look in her eyes and I panicked. But it wasn't fear. It wasn't hurt. It was a vengeful look that was almost murderous in its intensity.

I turned and ran out the door. I ran through the yard and down the street until my lungs burned and my eyes watered and my legs cramped. I didn't know where to go or what to do or who to call. I ran behind the Jiffy Lube down the street and I sat down and cried. I wept uncontrollably. I was a fucking joke, a failure, a complete menace to society. I had just hit my girlfriend twice. I was a wife beater. I was guilty of domestic violence. I was a disgrace to my family and a high school dropout and a low bottom drunk.

I deserved to die.

The woman cop listened while I poured out my heart about what had happened. I cried while I talked and I told her how sorry I was. She nodded and said she knew.

Time passed and after a while, I couldn't cry anymore. I couldn't talk anymore. I couldn't bear the thought of having to be me anymore.

The officer left the room and I was alone once again. I was tired. I was tired of this life, tired of these fights, tired of trying to be something I wasn't.

The officer eventually returned and when she did, she told me I was going to jail.

I told her I knew.

She handcuffed both of my hands again and led me to her car. I got in the back seat and looked up at the mountains as we drove towards the jail.

God how I hated those mountains.

Selected Essays, 2004-2005

"Oh where have you been my blue eyed son?"

Bob Dylan, A Hard Rains Gonna Fall

March, 2005

Without vodka it hurts.
 I haven't been to an AA meeting in a while and I guess the "pink cloud" from rehab is finally dissipating. My problems are forty-three days older, but still just as real as they were the day that I walked through doors of Hazelden. They haven't gone away and they certainly haven't become any easier to deal with. But I suppose that's part of the process.

I can't seem to stop thinking about the way things would have been had I made some different choices in life. I close my eyes and think back to the time when I was engaged, to the time when I had written my own version of a storybook romance. I had a ring and a way to propose and a plan and an amazingly beautiful girl who could cause time to stop when she smiled. I had love and lust and fun and a thousand butterflies flitting around in my stomach. But though it hurts to admit it, things have changed now and I find myself walking the streets of Chicago alone, save for my memories of better days. I hear the words of Tennyson echoing in my mind, "Tis better to have loved and lost...", but question the verity of his statement. I can't help but wonder if I would have been better off never having to go through this at all.

I've been waiting for time to do its job and heal these wounds, but still the pain persists. My hangovers are gone but my head still hurts. I spend my time trying to sort out the pieces to a puzzle that I've never even seen a picture of. I don't know my life without vodka. And I haven't been able to put her behind me.

I feel like I stopped to catch my breath and life kept going and when I started moving again everything had changed. I scan the crevasses of my mind for memories, the kind of memories that last a lifetime and make one miss a person or a feeling or a day or a kiss more than one could ever admit. I search for the kind of memories that have entangled themselves in my dreams. Memories that have woven a blanket of sadness under which I sleep. I try to look at pictures and can't. I sometimes call and hang up. I try to be tough and unaffected, but find that most of the time I am soft and afflicted. I find that although the lifestyle I am living now is somewhat fulfilling at times, when the sun goes down and I am alone with the dancing shadows of the moon's pale light, I am lonely and sad and cheerless.

I miss the little idiosyncrasies that made up my adaptation of true love. I miss how I used to be able to sit and stare at her for hours. I would capture the perfect, flawless image of her beauty and embed it deep in my mind so that when I went to sleep that evening, her image would be the last thing I saw. I miss catching the essence of her perfume on the wind and feeling myself light up with excitement that she might be near. I miss being able to be sappy when I felt like it, being able to cry for no reason, and being able to act mad when I wasn't just to get a rise out of her. I miss not having to explain why I felt the way I did about certain things, or why I have a scar on my arm and under my chin, or why I have a daughter. I miss having someone to impress when I would get the answer right on Jeopardy or Millionaire. I miss waking up in the middle of the night for the sole purpose of making sure she was in bed next to me.

I miss having someone to spend Sunday nights with and hate having a "case of the Mondays" alone. I miss the little bit of consistency I had in my life and I miss it every minute of every day.

In rehab, I was told that quitting drinking was the easy part and that it's figuring out how to live life without vodka that's hard. I couldn't fully understand that at the time, but suddenly it's become clear to me.

Without vodka it hurts.

July, 2005

Six months ago, when I made the decision to get on a plane, fly to Nowhere, MN to spend twenty-eight days reprogramming my entire way of thinking, I had no idea what I was getting into. I knew it would be rough, though, and I knew that things would change. I knew, rather, I hoped that people would start to see me in a different light. But what I didn't know, what nobody told me before I boarded the plane, what Hazelden had strategically left out of their marketing brochure was that, eventually, I would have to deal with all of the things that I had been running from for years. And I don't just mean the bills and the dry cleaning, but the feelings that I had pushed off and over to make room for "just one more." I had to reconcile with friends who, over time, I had replaced with mixed drinks and flashing lights, and I had to pick up my shovel, resist the urge to beat myself over the head with it, and begin to dig out.

But talking about digging out and actually digging out are two different things entirely. So I find myself sitting here, shovel leaning against the computer, as I type using commas and periods to bring some sort of semblance to my otherwise disorganized life. I write with an elusive purpose, yet a purpose nonetheless. I try to paint a self-portrait with brushstrokes dipped in nouns, verbs, and the occasional f-bomb in hopes that when I step back to take a look at the picture I created, I might be able to make a little more sense out of it.

Writing has been therapy for me. It's allowed me to begin to channel the anger I feel into a more positive direction, and I don't hold back even though sometimes I want to. I feel like writing is my way of admitting to the world that through car chases, bottles, blunts, pills, jail cells, fights, and Tupac's role in all of it, I became who and what I am. I've been an embarrassment and a lost cause and a train wreck, but at the same time I've been a role model and a big brother and a father. I've gotten lost about six hundred times while I've tried to navigate my life, but somehow I've managed to always make it back, or close enough to back, to where I'm supposed to be.

I think about all the things that I've gone through in my life and it makes me laugh and cry and strive to do better. I take long walks with the Marlboro Man because even though he's killing me softly, he quietly listens.

And sometimes, that's all I need.

July, 2005

When life gave me lemons, I made lemonade. And then poured an entire bottle of vodka in it. And although the concoction I mixed up was good at the time, I now realize it was actually the hemlock that was going to kill me. Unlike Socrates though, I wasn't drinking it for any sort of noble purpose. I was traveling through life with my head in the clouds and my feet never really touching the ground because alcohol altered my reality. It altered it to the point that I forgot what life was, what life is.

A gift.

Because the lives we lead, which are sometimes fun, sometimes hard, and sometimes Oscar winning, are our own unique gifts. It seems that I'd gotten my present from God, shook it around, put it up to my ear and listened to it, then put it down because, for a long time, I was too afraid to open it.

Before I could open it I needed a crutch, an alibi, a place to feel welcomed on a Saturday night so I drank buckets of moonshine. While I spent most of my days in euphoria, the real world was still spinning round and round. People were falling in love, out of love, laughing, crying, mending, and feeling real life the way it was intended. Our pain, our joy, our broken hearts, and our broken ways all define our journey. Our pain allows us to have our joy, our joy allows us to be in positions to have our hearts broken, and our broken hearts put mileposts on the maps of our lives. It's all connected and it's all intertwined and it all predicates our next crucial moment.

Dean Koontz once wrote, "Pain is a gift. Humanity, without pain, would know neither fear nor pity. Without fear, there could be no humility, and every man would be a monster. The recognition of pain and fear in others gives rise in us to pity, and in our pity is our humanity, our redemption."

Getting sober allowed me to finally find the pity within myself so that I could, consequently, give that pity to myself, inadvertently finding redemption in my own humanity and allowing myself to realize, once again for the first time, that life is a gift.

Today, I think, I will continue to open my present.

April, 2005

I don't think it's true that time heals all wounds. I think that time heals most of them, but chooses to leave a few of them behind to inflict pain every so often. I think that time uses open wounds to remind us of where we came from, what we've been through, and who we are.

Not too long ago I went to visit my parents, something I don't seem to do often enough. While I was there I spent time going through boxes of things that I had saved from high school. Memorabilia from simpler times, trinkets that brought little smiles as I thought about where I had gotten them, pictures of a youth lost. It was a trip down memory lane that I hadn't taken in a while and the outcome was bittersweet.

Memory lane is a dangerous place for me to go sometimes because the aftermath is usually filled with nostalgic days of soul searching. I don't know why things are the way they are right now. Why my daughter grows older in my absence, why my fiancé is about to marry someone else, why I have to Google my biological father to find out whether or not he's dead. I long for things to go back to the way they were. I yearn for second chances and opportunities and silently plead with God to give me a do-over. I write to try and find clarity, but I find myself writing in circles, coming back to the same things, the same topics, no closer to closure.

I want to scream at The Italian Job and tell her that I'm sorry, that I'm so terribly sorry. I reread the things I've written for her, about her, and I realize I can't make it any clearer. I have said what I've wanted to say in the most profound, honest way I know how and I suppose my answer lies within her silence.

I want to tell my daughter that the rollercoaster ride is almost over and we'll be able to kick it on the tea cups really, really soon. I want her to know that her dad, her imperfect, flawed, shell shocked father will fight tirelessly until his princess can rest easy by his side. I want to tell her that I'm turning my failures into stepping stones to bridge the gap between us. I want to tell her that I love her, that I need her, that I think about her every day that passes.

Memory lane is tiring and after walking down it for so long, I think it's time to stick out my thumb and catch a ride somewhere else.

Anywhere else.

April, 2004

I've always wondered why Clark Kent never told Lois Lane that he was Superman. I guess it just never made sense to me. Here was this guy, the self heralded "Man of Steel", God's gift to civilization and he longed for an ordinary girl as if he was an ordinary man. We all knew that he could have her. We all knew that all he had to do was fly to her house and take off his cape and all that he yearned for would be his. You see, Superman possessed what every man longed for. He had power and honor and fought for truth, justice and the American way. He had a secret that freed him of the tyranny of being human, but he never told her.

I think it drove me nuts because I could only wish to have a secret like that, a secret that gave me everything I'd ever wanted. Instead, my secrets only amount to felony charges, having a soft spot for chick flicks, and finding solace and comfort in the soft white glow of a Word doc.

The written word. Words that are written. Anyway you put it, it still spells release. But the irony of writing one's life stories is that the writing continues even when you don't want it to. There's no magic eraser that's big enough to get rid of the chapters I don't like. But hey, what's a good book without a cop, a girl, a crime, an obsession, a conflict, and an anomaly. I guess I took the road less traveled only to find out that I really wanted to be on the beaten path

I miss the innocence I had early in my life. I miss Sunday nights with Walt Disney. I miss having a crush on Haley Mills. I miss TGIF, Steve Urkel, Blossom, Webster, Vicki, and DJ Tanner. I miss orange cars that could jump lakes, black Trans-Ams that could talk, rich white guys that adopted poor black kids, and invisible jets. I miss the bliss that comes from the ignorance of not knowing what the result of my actions would be. I miss my first bike wreck, my first visit from the tooth fairy, my first kiss, and my first detention.

I miss everything that once defined my innocence. Before the corruption of broken marriages and the corruption of broken homes, I was whole, a boy with the enthusiasm of a firecracker who wanted nothing less than all the world had to offer. I had high expectations and high morale and I'm pissed because someone took it all away. I never gave anyone the right to take away my innocence; it was stolen, leaving me nothing more than a mere shadow of what I used to be. But life goes on, the wheels keep turning, the elevator keeps going up, the sun keeps rising, and I keep going over the same crap in my head.

My epiphany is long overdue.

The Italian Job

"Relationships are like glass. Sometimes it's better to leave them broken than try to hurt yourself putting it back together."

Author Unknown

I'm not sure who said it first, but I'm saying it now. Breaking up is hard to do.

Yes, I know its cliché and yes, I know it's a catchy 60's pop song, but seriously, breaking up is kind of like that story from the news a while back about that hiker that had to cut off his own arm with a dull knife after getting it stuck under a rock in the wilderness—you know you need to do it to survive, but it's going to hurt like a motherfucker.

When I broke up with Haley's mom in 1999 it was the relationship equivalent of an atomic bomb. I found myself, quite literally, homeless and somewhat toxic once we finally parted ways. There were enormous fights and police involvement and bitter tears and by the time it was all over with, I was on a Greyhound bus with a loaded gun in my backpack (a story for another time) heading east from Colorado. It took a big toll on me at the time and still now, ten years later, I can feel the residual effects.

Breakups have this way of molding the idea of what you think the next breakup will be like. We have this innate ability to lie to ourselves. We think that the most recent breakup we've endured is the worst breakup we could possibly be involved in and then, inevitably, we find ourselves going through another one and contemplating drinking the Drano underneath the sink.

It was early 2004 when my fiancé , who I lovingly refer to as The Italian Job, and I parted ways. The actual breaking up process was the proverbial death by a thousand cuts and it really wasn't all that surprising, given the way I was partying, that it ended the way it did.

I handled the breakup by vowing to do two things. The first item on the list was to drink myself into a virtual world in which I felt no pain and was void of all things wholesome. It was easy enough, though, given the fact that I was well on my way to doing it long before the breakup had actually occurred anyway. The second undertaking, the one that would take a bit more planning and scheming, was to find a way to hook up with her a few more times. It was the typical gorilla-like beating of the chest and ridiculous maneuverings and conniving that go along with trying to win back the woman that one loses. I was on a mission to prove to her that her choices were ill fated, that breaking up with me even though my addictions were single handedly ruining the very infrastructure of our relationship was wrong. I wanted to be with her again, but it was for all the wrong reasons. I wanted to show her new man "who the man" really was. I was pissed off and angry because I couldn't blame her for our relational demise and as much as I wanted to hurt her for hurting me, I think I really just wanted to make everything right again.

Not surprisingly, the first task was going well and I was doing my best to polish off a bottle of Effen vodka a day. I was successfully altering my reality to thwart the pain that was lurking just beneath the surface and I don't think I could have felt anything close to a feeling even if I had wanted to. But the second task I was trying to check off of my list, the part where I was supposed to plot and scheme a way to hook up with her a few more times, was backfiring and beginning to put some strain on my sanity.

Looking back, I think that I thought that I could detach quite a bit easier than I really could. I underestimated the power that time can hold on one's heart. Four years was a long stint when compared to any of my previous relationships and as much as it stung to admit it, I loved her in a way that I hadn't loved anyone before.

Breaking up with her was catastrophic for me. It rocked my world as if Atlas himself had dropped it. I felt like someone had punched me in the gut and I was doubled over and gasping for air that was nowhere to be found. I thought about her every time I was alone or sad or when the music to the party had finally stopped playing. I played the "what if" game and replayed the day that I broke up with her over and over in my head.

It was autumn in Chicago and the familiar colors of October lined the streets of the Southwest suburbs. The air held promises of colder nights in the upcoming weeks and the few leaves that were left on the trees were losing their fight to hang on. It was a Friday evening and I had decided to take The Italian Job's car over to my friend Tommy's house. He and I had gotten into a pretty regular habit of drinking into the wee hours of the morning and I was content with another Friday night of tailored inebriation.

I drove down the street and as I neared his house my cell phone lit up and with The Italian Job's familiar number illuminated across the screen. I hit the green answer button and said hello.

And in one instant, my whole life changed.

"I can't do this anymore." she said, her voice cracking a little.

I didn't understand what she meant. I mean, how could I? I had never in a million years imagined a future without her. This type of thing just didn't happen to us. We were engaged. I gave her a ring. I asked her the question and she gave me the answer. Yes.

"Do what?" I asked.

"This, you, us."

My stomach tightened up and I instantly wanted to throw up. What the *fuck*. I didn't even know what to say. I couldn't even think straight enough to give her a logical reply.

"Are you serious?"

"Yeah." And her voice trailed off into the expanse of time between us.

I've replayed this part of the conversation in my head thousands of times. There were so many things I could have said, so many things that may have changed the outcome. I could have begged and pleaded for another chance. I could have said that I was sorry, that she was right, that I needed to change.

But I didn't. Instead I was stubborn.

"I'll leave the keys in the car outside Tommy's house."

"Fine" she answers.

"So that's it?" My voice is ripe with indignation.

"Yeah, that's it" comes the reply.

But there's no anger in it. Her reply is filled with a sort of desperation. It's filled with sadness and heartache and the grim realization that if she doesn't end this relationship, that she won't be able to move forward.

"Well...bye, I guess..."

I make the few turns that are left before I arrive in front of Tommy's house. I stop the car. I sit there. I stare off into the distance and I wonder if this is really happening, if this is real. I convince myself that it's not and I just need to play this situation out. I convince myself that I need to be a hardass, that I need to go with the breakup plan so that I can show her, so that I can really show her, what a horrible decision it was.

I left the keys in the ignition and headed inside Tommy's house. I just wanted to drink. It was ironic I guess, how alcohol was the reason for, and solution to, all of my problems. Even then, amidst the crumbling of my small, insignificant universe, I couldn't identify the damage I was doing by seeking out alcohol instead of a little humility.

Downstairs in Tommy's basement I told him what had just happened. He looked surprised. I looked sad. He gave me a beer. I drank it. I got another one. I drank that one too. And little by little, my problems hurt less and less.

After an hour I walked to the window and looked outside to where the car was parked. It was gone.

She was gone.

We were gone.

The next day was Saturday and I didn't call. I should have called.

She didn't call.

I didn't call.

On Sunday morning she showed up at my house with an SUV and a suitcase. She was cordial, methodically packing up her things and placing them into the suitcase.

I was hung-over and trying to pretend that I wasn't bothered by seeing the love of my life getting ready to leave me forever.

But then I started crying and once I started I couldn't stop. I begged and pleaded and asked and demanded and implored her to please, please, please, stop packing. Please stop packing. Please don't go because I loved her more than I loved life itself and without her my life would be vacant.

But she doesn't stop.

She doesn't stop.

And I'm alone.

Half of the closet is empty and the barren hangers sway ever so slightly. It's quiet and I look around the room and see her in everything I look at.

I want to die. Without her I want to die.

She was an amazing girl and I was a fucked up boy and I let her get away.

It still hurts sometimes but life has gone on. I've heard that she's getting married this summer and that she seems to be happy. I sometimes wonder if she remembers all the time we spent together, but I'm always too afraid to ask.

Because I don't know what to do if she doesn't.

The Bridgeview Chronicles

"If you're going through hell, keep going".

Winston Churchill

The thing about breakups is that it almost always seems that the guy involved in the breakup tends to take it much less gracefully than the girl does. The guy usually has to readapt himself to the mundane chores he was somehow able to pass off throughout the course of the relationship and the first month or so spent in the single lane is used figuring out where the dry cleaners and the dish soap are.

At least that was the case in my situation.

After The Italian Job moved on to graze in finer pastures, I was left to fend for myself in a two story, makeshift apartment in the Chicago suburb of Bridgeview. The only pieces of furniture I owned were a hand-me-down bed from Tommy that dated back to his days in junior high, two Wal-Mart barstools, a bookshelf that looked like a strong breeze could destroy it, a television stand I managed to acquire from The Italian Job's parents, a desk that never had anything on it, a large and very broken thirty-six inch TV, and a piano. The piano was my favorite item, but since I didn't know how to play it (evidently the drinking I was doing must have negated the five years of lessons I had taken), it didn't do much but sit there gathering dust.

Because the house was so sparsely decorated, the only room that got any use was my bedroom. It was there that the broken thirty-six inch television sat on top of the stand and since the big TV was broken, I had placed a working thirteen inch television on top of it. (Before I actually owned a working television that sat on top of a non-working television, I found it hard to comprehend why one would do such a thing. But once I found myself in possession of such a large non-working television, I found that it was nearly impossible to just throw it out. It was like I was holding on to the idea that one day, like cancer suddenly leaving the body of a sick grandmother; the television would begin to work again.)

The worst part about it was that the working television only got two channels, one of which was Telemundo, the primary Latino broadcasting network. Telemundo was great, but it just wasn't for me. It wasn't that I had anything against Telemundo itself, after all, there were a variety of interesting "shop till you drop" shows in which unbelievably good looking and entirely flawless Latino women ran up and down grocery store isles frantically grabbing products off the shelves as the audience yelled things like "Get the ssoooaaaapp!!!" in Spanish. It was just that I couldn't speak Spanish and I didn't understand a word they were saying. Needless to say, "useless" was the decorative theme of my apartment.

The location of this particular apartment wasn't exactly ideal either, especially when you factored in the reality that I was a car-less, single, twenty-something working in the city. But every morning I would get up, usually late, shower, dress, and make the treacherous trek to bus stop. But before I could leave the apartment, however, I would have to hide any valuables that I happened to have lying around. It wasn't because I had such a wide variety of precious jewels or exorbitant amounts of cash stashed under my mattress though; it was because I had kicked in the door after locking myself out a few weeks prior, thereby making it impossible to lock my own apartment.

It was a two block walk to the bus stop where every morning of the workweek I would catch Pace bus number 385. The bus would maneuver me through the suburbs down Cicero Avenue, past Ford City shopping center and Maxwell Street Hot Dogs, and eventually to the Orange Line station at Midway that took me into the city. It was my normal routine and it was normally absent any sort of exciting event. Absent, that is, until the day I met Screaming Bike Guy.

The street corner where I would wait to catch Pace bus 385 was located at an intersection at the bottom of a big hill that ran over a collection of freight train tracks that fed into the city. It was a favorite spot of the neighborhood kids, and on most days one could witness children peddling themselves into a speed-induced bicycle euphoria. I noticed that, from the looks of it, if one of those kids were to peddle as fast as he or she could, starting from the top of the hill, it was quite possible he or she could achieve the speed of sound by the time they got to the bottom. And that, my friends, is precisely what Screaming Bike Guy did every single morning.

Screaming Bike Guy was a man that just sort of appeared one day out of the clear blue. He looked to be in his fifties, a stark contrast to the young kids that usually populated the hill, and he would ride his vintage ten speed bicycle like a kamikaze bomber at such a high rate of speed that on some mornings I couldn't tell if it was actually him, or just a figment of my imagination.

The thing that struck me as odd about Screaming Bike Guy was that after he had traveled about half way down the hill he would acquire a look on his face that was a cross between the proverbial "deer in the headlights" look, and the look a pyromaniac gets when he sees fire. It was a crazed look, a look that said, "Don't talk to me, I'm crazy." It was at that point; about halfway down the hill, a point which I came to believe was close to sheer nirvana for him, that he would let out a passionate cry that was not unlike the one that came from the mouth of Chewbacca. And the first time I witnessed this heralded feat I think I wet myself with pleasure and realized that, perhaps, this is what I had been missing in my life.

Once his primordial scream had been let out to his satisfaction, he would continue gaining speed until, by the time he was nearing the bottom of the hill, he would be traveling so fast that it would seemed like he was no longer even riding his bike. He looked to time warping, zipping through the time/space continuum like the main character in the movie *Jumper*. As the hill came to an end, and while he was still traveling at warp speed, he would have to execute a perfect, complete nincty degree turn to avoid being flattened by the morning traffic.

As I watched from my spot at the bus stop across the street from Screaming Bike Guy each morning I noted that the ninety degree turn that he executed everyday was virtually impossible. But not impossible as in unbelievable, impossible as in physically impossible. To go from the monumental rate of speed that he had reached while careening down the hill directly into a ninety degree turn seemed even more impractical than Mike Tyson singing bass in gospel choir. Regardless of what I thought, though, each morning he would do exactly that.

And so it went. Morning after morning, day after day, rain or shine, snow or sun, Screaming Bike Guy screamed and time warped his way down that fateful hill. He became a morning ritual for me, like shaving or throwing up or drinking coffee or brushing my teeth. I looked forward to the show and on the days I didn't see him, I would wonder if he'd finally met his demise.

One morning, as the cold wind and snow of December threatened to turn me into a human snow cone, Screaming Bike Guy performed a feat that will be forever etched in my mind. It was on that morning, unlike the others, that there was a car stopped at the red light at the bottom of the hill, exactly where Screaming Bike Guy had to make his hair splitting turn. He was in the post scream portion of his ride, but by the time my brain registered the imminent danger that was awaiting him, it was too late. Screaming Bike Guy seemed seconds from certain death! It was as if I was about to bear witness to what would happen, as my old man used to say, if the immovable object was hit by the unstoppable force.

The driver of the vehicle was oblivious to the fact that Screaming Bike Guy was about to hit his car. But then, just as the driver of the vehicle began to sense his lurking misfortune, it happened. Screaming Bike Guy started his ninety degree turn a fraction of a second early and, while passing the car in a frenzy of commotion, managed to stick out his neck and yell "HELLO!!" at the top of his lungs into the driver's side window. The driver, petrified yet quite unsure of what had actually just occurred, depressed his accelerator causing the car to lunge forward and then immediately slammed on his brake, thereby making his car to rock back and forth violently.

I stood across the street shivering from the cold with every muscle in my body tensed from the near disaster. The light changed green and the driver made his turn, a look of dismay on his face as he passed in front of me. Screaming Bike Guy was just a speck in the distance by then, but as I stared after him, I silently wished him Godspeed. He was a good man, that Screaming Bike Guy. But like all good men, it was only a matter of time before he was gone.

Screaming Bike Guy, this is for you.

The Happy Days of Cheers

Woody: Jack Frost nipping at your toes, Mr. Peterson?
Norm: Yeah, now let's get Joe Beer nipping at my liver.

From the television series Cheers, 1982

No matter where you live, no matter what town you go to, it's a pretty safe bet that you'll find that each city in America has its own version of the bar known as Cheers. Somewhere in each town sits a weathered barstool where you'll find various versions of Sam, Woody, Cliff, Diane, and Carla hurling insults back and forth over lacquered oak bars through the smoky Marlboro haze. And although the banter will probably be noticeably less witty and the accompanying lifestyles noticeably less interesting, the beer will still be cold and the advice will still be free.

As I bounced from one apartment to another during my early twenties, I found myself living with an attorney. I extracted a considerable amount of joy from the irony of the situation given my lengthy criminal background, and felt that I had somehow managed to shake the long arm of the law's hand in a truce.

The attorneys name was Tom, or Tom Tough Guy as we liked to call him due to the alter ego that came out during his periodic episodes of inebriation. He was the brother of my friend Tommy's girlfriend, and it was because of this connection that we found ourselves living together in the first place.

Tom Tough Guy worked in the city or "downtown" as it's referred to by suburbia's inhabitants. He had responsibilities and appointments and a jam packed Outlook calendar, so it wasn't all that uncommon to see him shaking his head as he passed me sleeping on the couch, clutching a bottle of vodka, as he left for work in the morning.

I was unemployed for most of the time that we lived together and coming up with the $350 I needed to pitch in to satisfy my portion of the monthly rent was an ongoing struggle. But it wasn't an ongoing struggle because I was the victim of societal hard times or a flaw in the American economic system; it was only a struggle because every red cent I made seemed to have a way of ending up down my throat or up my nose.

I had recently managed to get fired from my job as a server for the second time and was quite sure that my days working in restaurants that employed the "ten second rule" were over. Not having a job left me with all sorts of free time to drink and pontificate on the complexities of life until the wee hours of the morning without many repercussions. I could tilt back each of the bottles of an eighteen pack of Miller Lite and smoke weed until I could come up with what I thought was a logically sound, well thought out answer to why something transported by ship is called cargo and something transported by car is called a shipment.

The Italian Job and I were together at the time, a miracle in and of itself, and so I did what any alcoholic, unemployed, degenerate with a fiancé would do: I mooched off her.

It was a great deal for me, that much is certain, but it lacked reciprocity. The engagement I had her gridlocked into allowed me to use the argument "it's our money" without fear of reprisal. And so, time after time, again and again, an exasperated and agitated Italian Job would pull out her pocket book and out would come a twenty dollar bill or two.

Although The Italian Job and I spent most of our time together, we still kept separate residences. It allowed us to still have lives outside of our relationship and, now that I think about it, gave her a much needed respite from the antics of my life.

Monday nights were nights that we most often spent separate and on more Mondays than not, Tom Tough Guy and I would head down to the local tavern for ten cent wings, one dollar beers, and twenty dollar hangovers.

The bar was called BJ McMahons and by this point in my life I had become more of a permanent fixture in that bar than the grimy, worn out tables that sat inside it. It had gotten to the point where it was getting hard to distinguish between where my apartment ended and where the bar started. But it was my haven, my refuge, my port of call in largely dysfunctional lifetime voyage.

BJ McMahons was glorious. It was one of the few bars that The Italian Job hated to go to. That was a definite strategic advantage for me because it always gave me an excuse to drink without her. I could invite her to go, but rest assured that she would answer in the negative. It was win/win for me. I didn't look like a jerk for not inviting her, and I didn't have to listen to her tell me not to drink so much all night.

On the nights when Tom Tough Guy couldn't make it to BJ's and when I couldn't stand one more second of staring at the outdated paneling of my late seventies style kitchen, I could always count my friend Kevin aka The Dutchman, to come my rescue.

Kevin and I were alike in a lot of ways, the most notable being that we found ourselves unemployed around the same period of time. It wasn't that we were void of ambition or too proud to work; it was just that our dreams and aspirations didn't involve waiting tables and delivering pizzas anymore.

Kevin was much savvier than I was when it came to scraping up cash to head to the bar with. He was notoriously good at cleaning out the garage or the basement and making a substantial amount of money by implementing his knowledge of eBay selling.

We ran a pretty good racket, he would sell useless junk for profit and I would mooch off of him, and on more nights than not, we would end up at BJ's trying to come up with our next get rich quick scam. As I write this years later I find it hard to remember what any of them were, but I do know that by 2AM we were absolutely convinced we had come up with the next Google, eBay, or Beanie Baby idea.

BJ's was a perfectly constructed fortress of Irish bliss. Dark and dingy, with a smell not quite discernable, but definitely there, it was home to wings so greasy they would mess your shirt every time you bit into one. The glasses were never quite clean, the tables never quite balanced, the darts never all tipped. The cook resembled a drunken sailor and always cooked with a cigarette hanging out of his mouth. The Golden Tee game's display was tinted a greenish color from repeated overuse and most of the bartenders were on their second or third failing marriage, a fact they would bring up anytime anyone would listen. The crowd was made up of left over hair band groupies and constructions workers and anonymity was freely available.

For the most part, the cocktail waitresses that were employed by BJ's left a little to be desired in terms of attractiveness. But, to remain fair and objective in my assessment, there was one particular waitress that acted as the exception to the rule.

Enter Jessie.

Jessie was a community college student who seemed to work almost every night that Kevin and I chose to feed our insatiable addictions. More often than not, she was working hard to keep our pitchers full and our egos inflated as we tried to plot and scheme our way to the guest list of Donny Deutsch's show, *The Big Idea*. She was moderately attractive, but as the night would wear on, as our beer goggles continued to alter our reality, her position on the proverbial hotness meter would steadily increase. Kevin, after surveying the rest of the barroom crowd, would eventually come to the realization that it was Jessie or a steamy night with Rosy Palm and his attention would begin to divert from me to her.

It was innocent flirting in the beginning. Dart games and drinks, rear end pinches, the romantic batting of an eyelash, but after a number of weeks, the innocent flirting led to a series of events that rendered The Dutchman legendary in my book.

It was a on a rare occasion, an evening when I had passed on the nightly invite to join in on the BJ McMahon's debauchery, that I could be found snoring peacefully on my oversized couch. I had gotten in the habit of sleeping there since my snoring had reached a decibel level so high it made any sort of adequate night's sleep nearly impossible for The Italian Job. She was sleeping in the bedroom, as was usually the case, and the night wore on somewhat routinely.

It was somewhere close to 2AM when I had the distinct feeling that someone was watching me. But before I could open my eyes and confirm what I was thinking, I felt a pair of hands grip my shoulders and begin gently shaking them. Scared completely out of my mind and ready to throw ninja moves in every direction, my eyes shot open and I was face to face with The Dutchman. He was standing above me with bloodshot eyes, his breath smelling of whiskey and beer, a goofy look on his face. He was swaying side to side ever so slightly, and it looked like at any moment he just might fall on top of me.

Now I'm no McGruff Crime Dog, but I do know a thing or two about midnight visits from my friends. Typically, they meant one of two things: someone needed money, or someone had died.

Kevin, slowly trying to formulate the words in his head, finally stopped swaying long enough to say, "I need to use your couch."

My couch? Who in the world needs a couch at two in the morning?

Although I was a bit confused as to why The Dutchman needed a couch, it was a simple enough request and one that I was prepared to accommodate. I mumbled something along the lines of "no problem" and retreated into the bedroom to finish the night next to The Italian Job. Fatigue took over and soon I was fast asleep, unaware of what I would wake up to in the following day.

The Italian Job and I had an early morning planned and Rico was coming over for breakfast at seven. Tom Tough Guy and his fiancé were leaving for work about the same time that Rico arrived and as fate would have it, there stood the five of us in the living room staring at the couch.

Right in front of us was a trail of shirts, pants, socks, and an apron leading from the front door over to the couch. And there, draped over the coffee table for the entire world to see were the Dutchman's boxers. Next to them on the couch, basking in the morning sunlight coming in from the living room window, lie The Dutchman and Jessie.

Thankfully, The Dutchman was covered up with a blanket but Jessie, wonderful Jessie, the BJ McMahon's cocktail waitress, was wearing a baby tee and boy shorts. Rico, Tom Tough Guy, and I all looked at each other, smiling ear to ear, realizing that we had just encountered a half naked woman in our home that wasn't any of our fiancés. Breaking the silence of that majestic moment, Tom Tough Guy somberly said, "This is the best day of my life."

Indeed it was. We didn't have much going for us at that point in life and finding a strange, half naked woman in our living room that fateful day was one for the record books.

The girls mumbled words under their breath that rhymed with the words "bore" and "hut," and proceeded to shove the three of us guys toward the front door.

We strained our necks as we tried to steal one last glance before we left and there we saw, ever so slightly, the corners of The Dutchman's mouth turn slightly upward into a contented smile.

Jailhouse Rock

"Half our life is spent trying to find something to do with the time we have rushed through life trying to save."

Will Rogers, Autobiography, 1949

I once heard it said that the most watched television show in penitentiaries across America is Cops. As I'm sure most people do, I found this fun fact to be highly ironic and a wee bit comical. But that's not to say that I don't agree with it.

It was in the late nineties when I found myself having to pay a debt to society by spending what I thought was a more than adequate amount of time behind bars. I had made a few decisions that the judge didn't find nearly as humorous as I did, and my penance involved a sentence of sixty days in the clink.

The county jail in the county that I had carried out my crimes in was a little less, okay *a lot* less violent than the one located at 26th Street and California Avenue in Chicago, but that didn't make me anticipate my stint there any more eagerly. It was a small jail located in a small town and most of the offenders were career drunk drivers with misdemeanor offenses. But to shake things up once in a while, or because the county I lived in seemed to evoke criminal activity, there was often a variety of Department of Corrections inmates that were incarcerated there awaiting charges before being transferred to state prisons. The DOC inmates admittedly enjoyed the time they spent in the small county jail much more than the standard penitentiary because the food was better, the beds a bit softer, and unbelievably, it had cable. The Standard Plus package complete with HBO.

Television in jail was, more often than not, the source of every argument, fight and resulting fat lip. And there was a television hierarchy that was followed meticulously. *Sopranos* took precedence over everything except maybe nudie shows and *Cops* was the winner against anything else. I found it odd that the county jail even had HBO in the first place. To me, it didn't seem all that wise to show a rowdy clan of convicted offenders an episode of *G String Divas* right before bed. But, far was I from being the king of that castle and so *G String Divas* and *Cops* it was.

Watching *Cops* in jail was an extremely engaging thing to do. Inmates from all walks of life would point and laugh and make snide comments about whichever backwards redneck happened to be running around Southern Kentucky in his beer stained skivvies while attempting to pee on car batteries. I always thought it would be wildly amusing to be watching the show only to recognize the person on the episode and the person you shared your cell with were one in the same. But unfortunately, this never happened.

Days in county jail tended to move pretty slowly and after a week of sleeping, I decided I needed to figure out how things worked. Life in jail operated on a different system than life on the outside did, and I learned pretty quickly that if my time was going to be spent in a manner that didn't require that I sleep with one eye open, I was going to have to figure it out.

I began spending more and more time outside of my cell and with the general population. I kept myself busy reading, playing chess and checkers, doing pushups, and trying to push the omnipresent question "When am I getting out of here?" as far from my mind as I could.

My careful observations of Cell Block D told me two things. The first was that a moderately short, stocky guy named JoJo seemed to run the show, and the second, well, the second was that I needed to be friends with JoJo if I was going to survive my time there.

JoJo was about the same age as I was at the time, right around twenty, and we both shared the same love of hip hop music and Brittany Spears' schoolgirl outfits. He was in the county jail waiting to be brought up on charges of check fraud and was looking at doing ten years hard time. He was a good guy though, or at least a guy I could relate to. He had a beautiful girlfriend that was waiting for him to get out and he hoped and prayed, to the same God I did, that the courts would find leniency and grant him a lesser sentence.

We forged a friendship in jail and before long we were sitting at the same table for meals and swapping stories as we unhurriedly passed our days. He told me why he was there, about trying to transport crystal meth in a stolen car from Florida. He told me about high end fake ID's and computerized check forging, about thousand dollar shopping sprees and sparkling diamond necklaces. He told me how he got caught. He told me and I listened and while the rest of the world went about its business, we did the best we could to make do.

Being that JoJo was a bit more adept to the ways of the penal system than I was, I gladly followed his lead while he taught me how things worked. In county jail, everything that could be played could be played for money. And much like many other areas of life, the person with the most money had the most power. Or maybe I should say that the persons that were owed the most money had the power. Dominos, poker, pinochle, chess, checkers, whatever it was, it was for money.

Due to the fact that the inmates weren't allowed to possess actual cold, hard, cash there was another monetary system that existed. It involved placing a dollar amount on meals, like say, five dollars for dinner, three dollars for lunch, and two dollars for breakfast. In addition to that, commissary came into play.

Commissary was the jail store. Once a week the inmates were allowed to place orders for things like toothpaste, soap, snacks, playing cards or any number of other items that could help take our minds off of the fact that we were doing time.

We played cards a lot because JoJo was quite a bit like Worm in the movie *Rounders*. He could do things like deal from the bottom of the deck or "stack it" to make sure I made the last pair for my full house. We set up games where people would get a mark of twenty dollars, and throughout the play we would add or subtract according to what they won or lost

We played games like Black Mariah, Follow the Bitch, Omaha, Texas Hold Em', Cincinnati, Chicago Low, Jacks or Better, Stud, Draw, and anything else that whoever was dealing could think of. We played from morning to night, breaking only for meals. We played until they shut the lights off and then we got up and played some more.

We won more than we lost, partly due to the strategic dealing of JoJo, and before long we had most of the general population owing us money. We sometimes ate three dinners and two breakfasts and had Raman noodle cups that would last us for weeks.

We were doing okay for ourselves, and because we ran the card games and most of inmates owed us money in some form or another, we found ourselves at the top of the food chain.

Most days were uneventful and card games and *Cops* episodes passed the time in a place where time seemed to have stopped. JoJo and I continued to cultivate our friendship; often times spending the hours we spent away from the poker table talking about our lives and missed loved ones. It was a strange dynamic when I think about it. Circumstances that one would normally find appalling and stressful had brought us together. We vowed to have each other's back if shit ever went down. We promised to write each other when we got out, to keep in touch, to do what we could to keep each other in our prayers.

I've thought about JoJo a lot over the years. I'm thirty now, ten years after he and I shared a cell and if I've done the math correctly, he should be out this year. I've prayed for him periodically, hoping that when he does get out that something will have changed, that his life will be filled with better influences and healthier choices. But one never knows.

I spent the majority of my life making poor choices and it wasn't until I finally poured out the bottle for good three years ago that things started to improve. Because, for whatever reason, I needed each drink I took to finally get to a point where I could quit.

I thank God for the days that I spent locked up with JoJo and even though it was just shy of two months, it was long enough to teach me some pretty important lessons.

Time is short, JoJo, and life is fleeting. We need to ride this motherfucker until the wheels fall off.

50 First Dates

"A man on a date wonders if he'll get lucky.
The woman already knows."

Monica Piper

After my fiancé Suzie and I had bid our farewells, mostly through the unbridled use of four letter words and the exclamatory middle finger, I found myself back on the dating scene. I suppose it was a good time to be back on the dating scene since I was twenty-five and reaching the age where older, wiser, more established people were supposed to be taking me more seriously. And also, I was nearing the end of my first year at my job, which was slowly becoming my career, and Rico and I had nestled into the high-rise loft condo that would serve as the backdrop for many blackouts to come.

But the dating scene was daunting. Rico kept telling me that one-night stands didn't constitute actual relationships and I kept telling him they did. I told him that one-night stands were exactly like real relationships, only faster. I could accomplish in one night what it took other guys a month to do. We met, went on a date, held hands, kissed, got drunk, fondled each other, had sex, went to bed, woke up, had second thoughts, broke up, and said our goodbyes. It was like dating with a high-speed DSL connection. There was more clarity and less waiting.

But while one night stands and a revolving bedroom door were fulfilling for a little while, like almost any good thing, they had lost their taste and my life was lacking flavor. I had followed the self-destructive course that many men before me had taken and used my newfound freedom to do everything that I couldn't do when I was shackled by the restraints of a relationship. I bought clothes my fiancé wouldn't let me buy, talked to girls she wouldn't approve of, hung out with guys she didn't like, stayed out later than was reasonable, and all in all, applied the type of reasoning that exclaimed, "I'll show you! I'll hurt me!"

In hindsight, it was foolish. In real time, it was a blast. Because there's always that sense of rebellion that goes along with doing things you couldn't do when you were with a certain person. There's this ridiculous sense of self-deception where you convince yourself that you are much better off without her or him, and that the situation was detrimental for you anyway.

So in keeping with my resolve to do anything and everything I had ever wanted to do when I was with The Italian Job but couldn't, I set my sights on the lovely Chatty Cathy.

I suppose I should back up a minute and say that one of the difficult things about parting with The Italian Job was that most of our friends were mutual. During our time together The Italian Job had introduced me to a number of people who had become lifelong friends, and when we finally threw in the towel and left the ring for good, it was hard for them to pick whom to follow out the door. Most of the guys went with me and the girls went with her, but once the girls that were attached to the guys that went with me got done grabbing their men by the earlobes, I realized I was fighting a losing battle.

For the majority of the time it was manageable. There were some parties that The Italian Job would attend and others that I would attend, but every once in a while there was an event, like going to Tommy's condo in Lake Geneva or a NYE celebration, and the gloves would come off and we would fight for who got to go.

The Italian Job won more than I did and I began to resent the way things were turning out. I had lost my fiancé who I had loved more than anything else in my life at the time, and now I felt like I was losing my friends. In my mind all bets were off and the traditional rules that governed friendships and the types of things that were acceptable within them were up for negotiation.

Which brings me to Chatty Cathy.

Chatty Cathy was a stunningly gorgeous twenty-one year old girl with flawless, olive skin and a smile that could stop traffic. She was bouncy and vivacious and made up of sugar, spice and everything nice that twenty-one year old girls are made of. She was driven and hard working and always smelled amazing and I wanted her. It seemed simple enough, boy entices girl and they date. But in addition to being gorgeous and driven, Chatty Cathy was the younger sister of one of The Italian Job best friends.

To me, dating her was absolutely allowed. There would be a few different rules and I would have to be more committed if I ventured down that road, but I was up for the task and willing to take a chance at whatever repercussions would follow.

It was the beginning of fall in Chicago and another Windy City summer was tragically nearing its end. Rico and I had been plotting and scheming a way to celebrate our new lives as free men when, like a manna from heaven, we stumbled upon an idea for a party that was so good that even Lindsey Lohan would have approved.

The theme of the party was Golf Pro's and Tennis Ho's. The guys would dress up like golfers and the women would dress like tennis players, that is, sexy, Anna Kournikova-like tennis players. And, because we lived in what I would call a "playground for adults," we had the perfect rooftop setting for the festivities to be held.

We began the planning and as the days turned into weeks, the party began to take shape. We sent out Evites to everyone we knew with instructions to pass them on to anyone else that might enjoy the festivities, and depended on good old word of mouth to do the rest.

As the date of the party drew nearer, Rico, Tommy, and I decided to head to the North side to pontificate the upcoming events over chips, salsa, and basketball sized margaritas. We went to a place called Caesars, a popular hangout for the twenty-one and younger crowd where one could order margaritas as big as big as a bus while perusing a roomful of woman that Papa Time had not yet destroyed.

We arrived at the restaurant, ordered our drinks, and after I had excused myself to hit the restroom, I ran smack dab into Chatty Cathy and a few of her friends. She invited me to sit down for a minute and we talked about their plans for the evening and the upcoming party. I invited them to come, hoping that the invitation didn't scream, "I'm a scumbag!" as loud as I thought it did, and exchanged phone numbers.

We talked for a little while longer and I announced that I should be getting back to my table. I said a quick goodbye, offered up a wink and a smile, and off I was.

Back at the table, Tommy gave me a look that told me I was rolling the dice on the whole "go out with your friend's little sister" idea. He seemed to have a premonition that I was planning on giving her a call, and he knew that when her big sister found out that Chatty Cathy was spending time with me unbeknownst to her, that it might set off some fireworks — big, Fourth of July style fireworks.

I mulled it over, taking his thoughts into consideration, but it just didn't make much sense to me. I knew that my motives were pure, well all right, maybe not pure in the whole white as snow sense, but I certainly wasn't planning on posting a ScrewTube video of her and I together either. I knew I was going to go forward with the whole deal, but I figured that as the old saying went, I was better safe than sorry. I gave the doorman of my building a picture of Chatty Cathy's older sister with strict instructions that if she ever showed up there mad, he was to hold her off until I at least had enough time to throw myself down the garbage chute. The way I saw it, it was either throw myself down the garbage chute or have her throw me off the balcony. So, garbage chute it was.

A few days after our run in at Caesars, I gave Chatty Cathy a call. Rico was going to be gone for the evening and I thought she and I could spend the night getting to know each other. I was kind of a romantic at heart and living in a city like Chicago offered an abundance of romantic options. And it wasn't about sex either, it was about that first night when neither of you really know much about the other person so in your mind they're still pretty close to perfect. It was about trying to find that little bit of magic that exists before the reality of imperfection sets in.

So I called her and she accepted and a few nights later, she was standing in my kitchen.

I had picked up some wine and I pretended I knew a lot about the vineyard it came from and after pouring two glasses, the reason why I would later dub her Chatty Cathy became copiously clear. She possessed the phenomenal ability to talk more than anyone I had ever encountered in all of my days on the earth. She talked as if her life depended on it, as if her very existence was tied to her ability to have a two-person conversation with only one person talking. It was as if she took one breath in the beginning of the sentence and didn't take another one until the following Tuesday. I was flabbergasted. I honestly didn't know what to do and I was running out of facial expressions to respond to her with. I resorted to doing long division and advanced mathematics in my head so at least I could give the impression that I was concentrating. I finally got a break when she lifted her wine glass to take a drink and I jumped on the opportunity to ask her if she'd like to take a walk by the lake.

Lake Michigan in the evening, on nights where the air is calm and warm, is one of the true wonders of Chicago. The summer moonbeams sparkle off the water and the majestic lakefront has been the setting of more than one first kiss over the years.

My condo was just across Lake Shore Drive and after placing a bottle of wine in a backpack; we made the short trek across the street. We sipped wine from little red plastic keg cups and walked and talked and laughed. She talked more than I did, of course, but we were having a good time and the awkwardness that accompanies every first date was steadily wearing off. Couples strolled past us. Bikers, joggers, and rollerbladers of all shapes and sizes whizzed by. At one point during our walk, about the time that we were getting ready to sit on one of the park benches to rest, two police officers patrolling the lakefront on bikes passed us. My stomach dropped when I saw them and I had the sinking feeling that the red wine in the red keg cup I was holding was going to give me more than a hangover. In hindsight, I probably should have picked a less conspicuous wine glass because the one I was flaunting seemed to have a flashing neon sign with an arrow on the side of it proclaiming, "alcohol inside." I wasn't sure what the rules of drinking on the lakefront were, but when the two officers pulled a U-turn and started heading back in our direction, I was quite certain they were exactly opposite of what I hoped they were.

In my opinion, first dates are rough enough by themselves, but they can be downright unbearable when you mix them up with a run in with Johnny Law. And although the alleged crime that I was certain I was about to get charged with was minor in comparison to what I'd dealt with in the past, there was a small yet extremely irksome predicament I was finding myself in. Chatty Cathy and I had yet to reach the part of the date where I would begin to reveal bits and pieces of my tainted past. It wasn't that I was hiding anything; it was just that prefacing my pick up lines with "this one time, when I got a felony" didn't really seem like the most equitable way to get to first base. So when I saw the two officers backtracking towards us, my internal emergency crisis alarm went off and I remembered that I still had two outstanding warrants back in Colorado. The only perceivable light at the end of the tunnel was that both of them were misdemeanor warrants and carried no threat of extradition. But it still didn't alleviate the fact that this situation carried the propensity to be extremely embarrassing.

Chatty Cathy and I continued to talk and I did my best to try and ignore the cops as they came closer. I'm pretty sure I even tried closing my eyes really tight and hoping I became invisible, but when I heard the sound of a kickstand hitting the bike path, I knew that I wasn't.

The first cop came up to me and asked me what was in the cup I was drinking. I didn't see the point in trying to fabricate a story and so I told him the truth. I'm not sure why I did though, I guess it was me picking the absolute worst time to try and start mending my broken ways. I had learned a long while back that when it came to run ins with the long arm of the law, honesty was the absolute worst policy you could rely on. In fact, I had learned that the only thing that honesty could really get you was three to five in an eight by ten.

Chatty Cathy was next to me fidgeting with her glass and I could see the look on her face changing as she weighed out the potential outcomes of this situation.

The police officer continued on to tell me that there were only certain places along the lakefront where alcohol was allowed and then he asked me if I was aware of that.

I didn't then, and still don't now, understand why cops do things like that, why they insist on asking questions that are noticeably and blatantly rhetorical, and wait for an answer.

I told him that I wasn't aware of that little fun fact and he proceeded to inform me that where we were walking was most definitely *not* one of the places where alcohol was allowed. He told me that he was going to have to write me a ticket.

I glanced over at Chatty Cathy who had just been summoned over to the grass about five yards from where I was standing. The other police officer was talking to her in a low voice and Chatty Cathy was giggling. It dawned on me that he was probably hitting on her, but at that point I was thinking that I needed all the help I could get.

I looked back at the cop that was standing in front of me and asked him if I could pour out the wine and he and I could just forget our little misunderstanding. He shook his head no and pulled out his ticket pad. I told him that since the plastic glass of wine I was drinking was now going to cost me seventy-five dollars, I was going to finish drinking it. He said fine.

The officer asked me for my license so he could perform the customary background check and my heart sunk. Because although I knew the warrants that I had back in Colorado weren't extraditable, I also knew that having Chatty Cathy hear the officer on the other end of the radio confirming that I had them was going to be pretty detrimental in itself.

I asked the cop if we could walk out of my date's earshot.

We walked a few steps away from Chatty Cathy and I began to explain the situation to the officer. I tried to talk to him like a friend, explaining that I'd done some pretty dumb things when I was younger, but that I had changed and was beginning to live a new life. I told him about the warrant situation and how it would come back from HQ as a non-serviceable item. He listened and nodded, searching my eyes for signs of prevarication, but seemingly found none.

After I had finished explaining my situation, I listened while he told me that although he could empathize with the plight of the single man as much as any other guy could, protocol was protocol and he had to go through with the exercise regardless.

I looked towards Lake Michigan and contemplated this news. I knew it could play out a number of different ways, but I didn't really know which way would be worse – revealing my not so honorable past to Chatty Cathy or having her think she was being lied to. Neither option really seemed all that desirable, and I could foresee the night taking a turn in the wrong direction rather quickly.

The officer's radio remained silent as we waited for the news to come back from the station. Chatty Cathy and the other officer continued to make small talk while I shuffled my feet anxiously. The minutes drug on as they always seem to when one is nervously awaiting news, when, quite unexpectedly, I heard the jingle of handcuffs, and the officer next to Chatty Cathy instructed her to put her hands behind her back.

I stared at her with complete disbelief as the letters W, T, and F flashed through my mind. Could this possible be happening? Is Chatty Cathy getting arrested and if so, what in the world for?

For a brief second I felt a sense of relief, like maybe this momentary diversion would cause just enough interference for the officers to forget about me. But it didn't make sense. Stare at Chatty Cathy and one could conclude that her worst crime, at best, was jay walking. So unless they had started putting out warrants for people that jay walked and ran away, I was pretty sure that cuffing her had to be some sort of mistake.

After about two short minutes both the officer and Chatty Cathy burst out laughing. The officer reached for his handcuff key and un-cuffed her while his partner cracked a smile. Evidently, even hard-nosed, law-abiding citizens like these two yahoos had a sense of humor. But what really irked me is that neither one of them knew the colossal cock blocking they were absentmindedly delivering. Because it was no sooner than the handcuffs were off of Chatty Cathy that the radio crackled with dispatch alerting them that I did indeed have a warrant. But it didn't stop there. No, in addition to confirming that I had a warrant, the woman on the other end of the radio said she couldn't tell which type of warrant it was, therefore, she was not able to advise the officer as to whether or not I should be taken into custody. She mentioned something about the system being down.

I knew that this posed a problem because the words that came out of the officers mouth after that were something along the lines of "let's go down to the station and talk about it." While I may not have known much in that stage of my life, I knew with absolute certainty that "talking about it," meant handcuffing me to a metal bench in a police station somewhere.

The officer took out his handcuffs and as I put my hands behind my back I looked over at Chatty Cathy. I really didn't know what to say to her at that point. I mean, what could I really say about being arrested on our first date?

In the most reassuring voice I could muster I told her that things would be okay and that this was all just a simple misunderstanding. I asked her to take the backpack off of my back and pull my keys out of my pocket. I told her she should just walk back to my condo. I told her that I would be home soon enough and that she should try to let Rico know what was going on.

The cop that was standing by Chatty Cathy offered to walk her back to the condo and I felt a little bit better about having to leave her. I told her I was sorry and she and the cop began walking towards my place.

I looked back out over the sparkling water of Lake Michigan, my hands behind my back in handcuffs and, for a brief second, I felt like I would never be able to escape my past. I had worked so hard to try and put my feet back on solid ground, but the reality of who I was—a criminal with a long and sordid past—seemed to surface every time it got the chance.

The paddy wagon showed up to take me to the precinct and I got into the back of it and sat down. I laid my head against the metal cage and slowly let out a long, deep breath. The paddy wagon began to move and I bounced around in the back, catching glimpses of the clear sky outside the small, shatterproof window. The moon laughed. The lake sparkled. And the more that things changed, the more they remained the same.

There's No Place Like...

*"The truth is that our finest moments are most likely to occur when we
are feeling deeply uncomfortable, unhappy, or unfulfilled. For it is only in
such moments, propelled by our discomfort, that we are likely to step out
of our ruts and start searching for different ways or truer answers."*

M. Scott Peck

April, 2007

The month of July begins to come to an end and August knocks on
summer's door. Time passes as it always has, sometimes quickly,
sometimes slowly, propelling me forward into a future that seems
undeniably uncertain. I struggle with my transition, missing the Second
City with each beat of my heart, silently counting down the days until
I can once again call Chicago home. I wander through the city of Atlanta
and feel like a visitor, a trespassing city boy stuck in a smorgasbord of
rural molasses. I absentmindedly search for love in the acquisition of
things, but find that the black hole inside of me has yet to get any smaller.

Evidently Mercedes doesn't make band-aids.

In the early morning hours as the airport begins to awaken, I sit
and think and type. I yearn for an emotional revelation, a sudden
calming of my animated subconscious. I hope and pray that with each
click of my Japanese keyboard that I might somehow find myself
closer to the solace that seems to have been lost in my move. I reread
things I've written about rehab and the early days of sobriety, words
that helped soothe the pain that radical change brings with it. I read the
struggle I went through and can still feel the tenacity I used to keep my
feet shuffling forward.

Still though, I am deeply uncomfortable.

Because even though long ago I vowed to never, ever live a life of
mediocrity, the sacrifice of comfort that comes with the pursuit of
happiness can sometimes be all too painful. Change can be all too painful.

In Atlanta, things move more slowly, time moves more slowly. I constantly think about where I am and where I want to be and come to the conclusion that I need to work harder, to work faster, to work longer. Because there are really only two fundamental choices in life: choosing to accept the way things are, or choosing to change them.

So I choose to change them. I choose to not give up, to not grow complacent, to accept change and antagonize it when I can.

Marylyn Ferguson once wrote "It's not so much that we're afraid of change or so in love with the old ways, but it's that place in between that we fear... It's like being between trapezes. It's Linus when his blanket is in the dryer. There's nothing to hold on to."

Right now, Linus' blanket dries and I contemplate spending the nickel and asking Lucy for some advice. I don't know the next move and the uncertainty of which direction I should lean has me catching a few punches on the chin. I'm discontented with where I am. I'm hungry. I'm restless. I feel the growl of the pit-bull inside me and my veins pulse with oxygenated blood. I attack the gym with a ferocity that had lately been dormant and hit the heavy bag until my knuckles bleed and my arms shake with exhaustion. I push myself through the pain, through the walls that stand before me, hoping, praying, wishing that I could fast forward to the time when I've grasped all that I've reached for. But I know that this thing, this life that has me laughing and crying and wondering isn't a destination, it's a journey, a long walk down an unpredictable road.

These last two and half years have gone by in the blink of my sometimes-black eye. I've been chasing my childhood around, never quite catching it, but chasing it nevertheless. I chase it because I miss it, because like so many others around me, I didn't know how good it was until it was gone, I didn't know how much it meant until it transitioned into a distant memory.

Change is hard and when I think about it, I know it always will be. There's comfort in habits, in familiarity, in the commonality found in friends. There's a part of me, of everyone, that knows that when Dorothy clicked her heels three times and spoke those infamous words, that she was absolutely right. There's no place like home.

Even when it's changed.

The History of Love

"Absence is to love as wind is to fire; it extinguishes the small and kindles the great."

Roger de Bussy-Rabutin

Chicago

The first time I saw the movie *The Notebook* I cried for an hour straight after it was finished. But I didn't feel all that unmanly doing it because, as it turns out, every guy in America that has ever been talked into watching that movie has done precisely the same thing. In fact, the man cry that follows every viewing of Nicolas Sparks' masterpiece has even prompted its very own term: getting Notebooked. As in, "she totally notebooked you!"

It's amusing to me how we all yearn for the fairy tale romance that guys like Nick Sparks dream up. We all hope to one day be like Noah Calhoun and Allie Hamilton and capture the magic of love while kissing passionately in the falling rain of sudden thunderstorm. But for most of us, that's all we get; a hope and a dream and a tear stained pillow after the cinema lets out.

But every once in awhile, every so often, we hear a story or meet a couple or see a pair of old folks walking hand in hand and our hope is once again awakened.

It was nearing the end of 2004 and although I didn't know it at the time, my lifelong love affair with vodka was about to be over. No matter what I tried, things continued to get progressively worse for me. I was in a serious amount of debt with no legitimate means of getting out in sight and everyday just seemed to bring a new onslaught of problems. Rico and I were still managing to live the highlife in our high-rise crib, though, so when he suggested that I tag along with him and his family on the yearly Caribbean Cruise, it was a no brainer.

But as December ended and we rang in 2005 with a fistful of ecstasy pills, life, as it turned out, had other things in store for me.

Off to rehab I went.

Now don't get me wrong, rehab was an amazing blessing for me, but it was so hard to see that at the time. Nothing puts a damper on a Caribbean cruise quite like a twenty-eight day stay in the Hazelden rehabilitation facility.

I emerged from rehab looking like the same person that had gone in, but the reality couldn't have been much different. I had just spent twenty-eight days learning that everything I did in my life all the way down to the fundamental ways that I tried to intellectualize my problems was wrong. I didn't know where I fit in anymore. I was supposed to be fixed, to be better, but all I felt was a profound sense of mystification, timidity, and the absence of self confidence.

I wanted to go on the cruise with Rico to show everyone that I was the same person and could do the same things and have just as much fun without alcohol, but deep down inside I knew that I couldn't. I needed to beat my problem and since I had finally been able to take the first step toward winning the battle, I decided I would have to gracefully bow out of the trip.

Rico understood, or at least he said that he did, and when the time came, he sailed the seven seas without me. It was oddly metaphorical. Rico and I had been friends for so long that I loved him like he was my own brother and for the first time in our lives, we were on ships that were sailing in separate directions. It was hard for me, harder than I ever led anyone to believe, because I felt like I had let him down, like I had let everyone down. I had tried so hard to walk the tightrope between success and failure, but my footing had finally faltered.

So off he went and off I didn't and after ten days of fun and sun and triple dirty monkey drinks, back he came. He was tan and excited and a little bit hung over, but there was something else, something about the way that he was carrying himself that had me wondering if there had been more than alcohol in his Mai Tai.

I had been on the couch in our condo watching reruns of *Everybody Loves Raymond*, the greatest television series of all time, when he waltzed in, evidently dancing to some sort of music that only he could hear. And from the second I saw him I knew something was up, but I was hoping it was the kind of something that went away with a good night's sleep and a couple of Advil.

He walked, danced, floated, across the room and sat down on our black leather chair and began to tell me about his trip. One very specific part of his trip. The part that sounded like mumble, mumble, girl, mumble, I'm in love, mumble, mumble, mumble.

He was saying things like "colors are brighter now", and "my life now has true meaning" and I think there was even a reference to wishing upon a star. He was giddy and capricious and whimsical and I was immediately just as jealous as the day of the break in when he showed up in those majestic Phantom in-line skates. As much as I hated to admit it, it seemed Rico was in love.

Now, it wasn't that I didn't want Rico to be happy or to be in love, but every guy who's ever had a best friend knows what happens when his boy slips, trips, and falls head first into the big mud puddle of love. It's the law of the jungle. "Bro's before ho's" is the mantra we live by, but only until a beautiful woman steps in and calls off all the bets.

I didn't want all the bets to be called off yet. I wanted my wingman to continue to be wingman and I was deathly afraid that this new girl, *The One*, as Rico referred to her, was going to infiltrate my life and commence stealing my best friend.

Less than a week passed since Rico had been home from the cruise and he was on a plane again, this time to the rainy gloom of the Northwest. The One had been living in Seattle for the previous three months and was about to make a move to the sunny beaches of Mission Viejo, California. The plan was for Rico to fly to Seattle, help her load up a U-Haul, and make the protracted voyage down the Pacific Coast Highway with her.

Rico left and I began to notice that it was getting harder for me to stay cynical about the whole situation. Rico exuded a boyish excitement that reminded me of my first days with Suzie, so who was I to act like the spoiled little brat who wasn't getting his way? Besides, the more that Rico talked about her, and he talked about her a lot, the more she was rubbing off on me. She sounded cool and beautiful and independent and the complete opposite of the last significant relationship that Rico had. Which was good because the last girl that he had dated I had fantasized about letter bombing on more than one occasion.

With Rico gone and with the word on the street having gotten back to the rest of the crew, Wayne and I mulled over his newfound romance while polishing off a pretzel trio at Bar Louie.

Wayne was just as skeptical as I was at first. We had both been witness to the blatant miscalculations of the Rico Romance Radar on a couple of other occasions, and suddenly I was remembering the last time that Rico came back from an exotic vacation with tales of island beauty queens. In fact, it was just the previous summer when Rico showed up tanned and hung over, boasting of his latest fairy tale romance at high seas. He successfully talked me into jumping in the car and driving five hours to Detroit in search of his fling. But when we got there, not only was the girl that was supposed to be my consolation prize for making the trip about as far from single and beautiful as one could be, we somehow got roped into moving her from one apartment into another. I mean, I don't even like moving people I know so you can only imagine the look on my face as I tried to fit her stained futon down a narrow staircase.

In the beginning, Wayne and I had about as much faith in Rico's ability to locate love as we did in the quality of a haircut given by the Flowbie. There was just no way that the relationship between Rico and The One would make it all the way back to Chicago.

Rico's first trip out to see The One lasted for five days. Just as they planned, he flew out to Seattle, loaded up the truck and drove for hours down the scenic coast of Americas left side. They stopped at Napa Valley vineyards where, over cheap wine and expensive cheeses, he told her stories about his pony tail days and the time he broke his tooth on his skateboard. He learned about her life, about her job, and how she had spent the majority of the last few years traveling the country as an occupational therapist. They talked and drove, laughed and drank, and by the time they finally unloaded her things into a beautiful home in southern California, Rico was one hundred percent, head over heels, crazy about that girl.

By the time Rico got back and replayed his trip for the thousandth time, I knew that I had to see this for myself. If my boy, my best friend, the guy who knew the exact number of the amount of women I had slept with, was admitting to being as in love as he said he was, well, I was just going to have to meet her.

Rico was already planning another trip out to California when I told him that I was coming with him. I explained that since he seemed to have finally found someone who could understand, or at least pretend to understand, the words that came out of his mouth after a few drinks, that I had to see and meet this girl for myself. That was one of the funny things about Rico. He had this innate ability to mumble like no one I had ever met in my life. He had this way of slurring all the words in a sentence together so that the outcome would be one, extremely long, three hundred syllable, rather impossible to understand word. I had actually been wondering if the whole time that Rico and The One were on their fateful journey down the West Coast, if she just nodded and smiled the whole time, never quite understanding a single word he said.

Rico was happy with the plan and after a few clicks and points on Priceline.com, it was off to California we went.

San Diego

There's something about Southern California that seems to speak to a part that's buried deep inside of all of us. Maybe it's the dream of having our name in lights, or the appeal of having a year round tan, or maybe it's something else, something more trivial that keeps us looking to the West for answers. Alison Lurie once said, "As one went to Europe to see the living past, so one must visit Southern California to observe the future." The One, it seemed, just might be that future.

We flew from Chicago to Santa Ana and it was good for me to get out of the city. I was a few months into sobriety and AA meetings and step work were beginning to take a toll on me. I wanted a taste of my old life for a minute, not the drinking and nonsense that went with it per se, but the excitement that it now seemed to be lacking. I was looking forward to my little getaway.

The flight was altogether uneventful and by the look on Rico's face, his excitement was building with each air mile we traveled. The One was meeting us at John Wayne Airport and the moment of truth, the time when I would finally bear witness to Rico's self proclaimed "One," was almost upon us.

Even though we'd yet to be introduced, I knew what she looked like because over the course of the last two weeks our condo had become a sort of strange shrine to her. Photos had appeared in places like the front of the refrigerator and in various locations around his bedroom, and there was even a picture on the back of the toilet in the bathroom. It was odd I think, to find myself peeing and staring at a picture of Rico's new girlfriend. I was always a little uncomfortable and even suffered a case or two of stage fright. And there were even a few times that I just plain had to turn the picture around.

The plane descended, landed, and minutes later we were taxiing down the runway to the gate. We deplaned, hustled through the airport terminal towards the baggage claim, me frantically trying to keep up with Rico who was in full sprint by that time. It was a bit like that scene in the movie *Home Alone* where Kevin's family runs through O'Hare in a panicked frenzy while trying to make their plane. It was a bit like that, but with less people there wasn't a security guard yelling at us just yet.

We rounded the last corner, me trying not to face-plant right before baggage carousel one, and before I even had a chance to catch my breath from trying to keep pace with Rico, I was face to face with The One.

The One looked even more beautiful in person that she did in her pictures. She was five foot eight with brown hair and green eyes and a body that could have inspired Juvenile's hip hop classic, "*Back That Thang Up*." She finally stood before me, present and accounted for in flesh and blood.

Rico barreled passed me and I was immediately in one of those awkward positions where the whole "third wheel" thing is exceedingly apparent. But as soon as she and Rico took a break from the world's most graphic display of public affection, she shuffled over, gave me a hug, and introduced herself. It was a cool moment, a prelude of things yet to come. We were from cities that were miles apart and under any other circumstances we would have never met. Yet here we were, surrounded by annoying travelers with designer baggage, about to embark upon a California dream together.

I got our luggage while Rico and The One pulled the car around, and fifteen minutes later we were driving down Highway 1 with the windows down and the system up. Rico and The One had completely forgotten that I even existed, but I didn't care because I could smell the ocean on the breeze. Life was good for a minute. In that moment I wasn't an addict or an alcoholic or a criminal with a lengthy rap sheet. I was just me. A boy with a best friend who found a girl in a California. And nothing, and I mean nothing, else mattered.

The drive from the Orange County airport didn't take long, and before I could even convince The One to stop in Laguna Beach so

I could try and fulfill my own romantic fantasy by tracking down Lauren Conrad from MTV's "Laguna Beach", we arrived in the Gas Lamp District. The city streets were lined with bars and people and the music overflowed into the patios as we walked by them. It was a beautiful California night and the air was calm and the partygoers weren't and every girl I looked at seemed like she was a magazine centerfold. It was a silicon playground of perfectly sculpted bodies and name brand style and I was immediately the happiest man west of the Mississippi.

We entered one of the bars and Rico did the Running Man and I did the Carlton and The One laughed and laughed until she almost choked on a cocktail cherry. It was good times and we danced until our shirts were soaked in sweat and the night wore thin. We danced until the stares that we had gotten from the rest of the club goers in the beginning wore off and we danced until we couldn't dance any more.

I left Rico and The One to their drinks and the endless sucking of face that they were constantly involved in and took a lap around the bar.

In the weeks and months preceding the trip an old high school friend and I had started talking again. She had been living in San Diego the last couple of years and our almost nightly catching up had turned into a Joey/Rachel sort of thing. She was fun to talk to and over the years we had ended up in the same bed once or twice, drunkenly fondling each other's areolas, but nothing romantic had ever really materialized. We were always just good friends. Good enough friends that I could talk to her on a nightly basis about being my interim girlfriend while I was visiting. I told her that it would be best for everybody, that since we were going to be running around sunny California with a couple who once had an hour conversation that consisted entirely of "I love you more. No, I love you more," that it would be imperative for her and I to forge a relational bond when I got out there. I, of course, would do my damndest to find a part time girlfriend while we danced the nights away, but on the off chance that I couldn't, she needed to be my plan B.

I didn't have to walk very far and there she was. The melodic undertones of Warrant's Sweet Cherry Pie were fueling a wealth of booty shaking in her that was screaming for an MC Hammer song. She was laughing and sweating and teasing old men with a plethora of moves that involved different variations of hip gyration.

She saw me and her face lit up with a smile that could have shamed the lights of Vegas. She ran to give me a hug. We embraced.

She felt good. I felt good. We were in California and we felt good and the night was warm and the music was loud. Plan B was there, Rico was there, The One was there, I was there, and although the dance floors were packed with people, all we saw was each other because friendships are like that. Sometimes they're so good that the rest of the world just ceases to exist for entire minutes at a time.

The dancing finally began to slow and the night began to segue into dawn. We were tired and sweaty, but happy to be with each other, happy to be in California, happy to see that what Rico and The One saw in each other's eyes seemed to be for real.

We left the bar and after a brief conversation in which it was decided that a burrito was the only celebratory feast worthy of an occasion such as the one we were experiencing, Plan B and I jumped into one car while Rico and The One jumped into another.

The fact that California is 47% Hispanic is extremely helpful when one embarks upon a journey to find the perfect burrito. The California night sky is lit up with different colors emanating from the bright neon signs that advertise things like "burritos as big as your head" and "burrito es muy grande" so it didn't take us long to find the spot that had claimed a special place in Plan B's heart.

We parked our cars and as we breathed in the smells of freshly made corn tortillas and guacamole, the four of us walked over to the small, run down taco stand. We got in line and I began to browse the menu, looking for anything that could quiet the rumbling of my empty stomach. After a minute or two, though, I became vaguely aware that there was a group of guys that were watching my every move. I glanced in their direction and it dawned on me that these guys could be stand ins for the entire cast of that show "Queer Eye for the Straight Guy." The loudest one, the one who looked exactly like the lead singer of White Snake, had long hair that was feathered in the front and was donning tight leather pants and slowly smoking a cigarette while watching me. He got up from his perch on the picnic table he was sitting on, walked over to me, took a drag of his cigarette and while he exhaled said, "You bitches in line?"

I didn't really know what to say to that question and judging from the beady-eyed look that was projecting from Plan B's face; it was obvious that she didn't know either. I think it was because of the way the guy had said it, similar to when someone who grew up in the seventies tries to use phrases they used to say when they were a kid but can't pull it off anymore.

I told him that yes, we were in line, and from the vibe this guy was giving off I couldn't help but think that he and his crew were waiting for wieners rather than tacos.

Miraculously, our food was finally prepared and the four of us got back into our cars and started to drive towards Plan B's house. We made our way down the streets of the darkened city, all the while salivating from the aroma of refried beans and rice. We drove past all night diners and lit up gas stations, past partygoers wobbling down the narrow sidewalks, and eventually into the neighborhood where Plan B lived.

It seemed like a nice neighborhood. There were palm trees mixed in with the streetlights and they cast spider-like shadows up and down the streets as we parked our cars and made our way around back to where her house was.

Outside her door, while Plan B fumbled with the keys, Rico and The One used the few moments of stillness to twist their tongues together yet again. I stepped back and sized up the house. Plan B had said it was small, but I was beginning to think that perhaps that was the understatement of the century. I remembered that a while back, Geico Insurance Company had a commercial where a husband and wife were seen happily interacting with one another until an ominous voice came on and said, "The marriage was built to last...but the house was built TOO SMALL!!" and the commercial would flash from scene to scene of the couple bumping into walls, the ceiling, and so on until the husband screamed, "I just want to make an omelet!!"

Well, that was where Plan B lived.

Plan B finally got the door open and we walked in to the kitchen/living room/foyer. And with the four of us now taking up all the actual living space in the entire house just by standing there, our gazes immediately settled upon the only two areas where one could potentially sleep. Plan B had a bedroom, but I use the term loosely since it was more like a curtained off section of the kitchen/living room/foyer.

The sleeping arrangements were going to be a bit like a sixth grade sleepover, but we were tired, it was late, and we were just happy to be together. We ate our burritos and tacos and tortilla chips and after we had cleaned up after ourselves, Plan B and I went to her bedroom while Rico and The One jockeyed for position on the couch.

I lay down next to Plan B, put my arm around her, closed my eyes, and minutes later I was drifting off into dreamland. My mind raced from one thought to the next, skipping back and forth between rehab, childhood, and Haley. I thought about where I had been and what I had gone through to get there. It had been a long, hard road, but I was starting to think that maybe there was a light at the end of the tunnel and maybe, just maybe, that light wasn't a freight train.

Plan B's breathing had fallen into a steady rhythm and it was nice to feel her so close to me. I'd been running a race by myself for quite a while by then, and I had forgotten what it was like to sleep next to someone I actually cared about. For the first time in a long while, I felt safe.

I fell asleep with a feeling of quiet contentment wrapping me like a blanket.

Minutes after falling asleep, I woke up to the sounds of whispering, giggling, and heavy breathing. Now, I'm not a super sleuth by any stretch of the imagination, but I have read enough Hardy Boy novels to put two and two together. So, when I woke up and heard the unmistakable sounds of heavy petting going on some three and a half feet from where I was sleeping, I found myself in a dire predicament. Because even though Rico and I had been involved in a number of embarrassing situations throughout the course of our lives that we swore we would never tell another soul, there were still some things about him I didn't want to know. Like, for example, what his "*Oh*" face looked like. So in the minutes that followed the startling discovery that I was about to get to know Rico and The One in a way that was far too intimate, I counted sheep and counted backwards and did everything in my power to fall asleep.

Although there was a bit of collateral damage that night, and I bore witness to a few scenes and some noises that will forever be buried in the depths of my medulla oblongata, it had been an amazing night, a true California dream.

Top Gun

The following morning after we woke, Rico and I decided to give the girls some time to do the things that girls do in the morning that make guys like Rico and I love them. We walked to the 7 Eleven convenience store down the street and the whole time we were walking I was looking at Rico and feeling slightly nauseous about the whole "*Oh*" face debacle. He was looking right back at me in a puzzling way and after contemplating it in my head for a couple of minutes; I decided that some things were better left unsaid. After all, there's really no heterosexual way to tell a guy that you find his low and throaty sex groan to be revolting. Because things like that should just never come up in some conversations.

We made it to the convenience store and while Rico fixed himself a cup of java, I rummaged through the aisles looking for something, anything that would help give me an artificial fix of energy. One thing I've notice about 7 Elevens' across America is that they are like the devil's medicine cabinet when it comes to energy. You can walk through any 7 Eleven in any state and put together enough ingredients to fuel your car for three, maybe even four miles. And that was a great thing for me. Fresh off the SS Rehab and I still had the addictive tendencies that got me there in the first place. I felt like I needed something, anything to alter my state of mind. I wasn't yet totally comfortable in my own shoes and if I couldn't have drinking and drugs anymore, well, maybe I could make a 7 Eleven concoction that could act as a substitute.

I settled on coffee, Red Bull, and a couple of brightly colored foil packages that appeared to hold some sort of pills inside. We paid for our purchases and walked back to the house to get the girls. They were ready and before long we were back in the car and heading towards downtown San Diego. To Miramar. To the place where dreams come true. To the place where Slider, Maverick, Goose and Iceman graced the sunny skies of Southern California with barrel rolls and dog fights in May of 1986.

To say that I'm a Top Gun fan is like saying Money Mayweather is just a boxer. For me, and Rico for that matter, Top Gun defined a certain part of our existence. We felt the need for speed and strove to live our lives outside of the lines. We identified with Maverick's quest for personal understanding and felt his pain when he lost his wingman. I hated to think about that, about losing my wingman.

We drove down the highway and I sipped my coffee, chugged a Red Bull, and popped a handful of pills from the package I had just bought. Things were good. Things were great actually. The wind was blowing and the sky was blue and the sun was shining. I began to feel happy. Really happy. Happier than I should have been. I suddenly realized that something strange was happening. I felt like I had just taken an ecstasy pill and was waiting for the roll to begin. I could feel my hair grow and my eyelashes move and from somewhere in the car there was the faint noise of buzzing electric. I looked around and then I realized it. The buzzing noise was coming from me! I had so much caffeine and over the counter cocaine in me that it was if I was electromagnetic! I'm quite certain that if I would have pulled off the road and peed, that right there on the side of the highway, a Redwood tree would have immediately sprung from the ground.

We drove a bit further and before long the downtown metro area announced itself with shimmering steel and glass. I was excited and from the looks of Rico, he was excited too. We were almost there. To the Holy Grail. To the Kansas City BBQ—the place where Goose plays Great Balls of Fire on the piano, where Maverick drowns his sorrows and after losing him, and where that infamous quarter drops into the juke box and it starts playing *You've Lost That Loving Feeling*.

We parked and walked down the street and there in front of me, just as I dreamed it one day would be, was the famous Kansas City BBQ. The front window of the bar held a neon sign bearing the words *Top Gun* and next to the entrance was a plaque immortalizing the days the scenes were filmed there. We walked inside and off in the corner was a majestic mural of the afterburners on two fighter jets that could have been painted by Michelangelo himself. The walls were packed with pictures of the filming, of Tom Cruz, of Miramar, of planes. There were tables and chairs and off by the bar, sitting there in all its glory, was the infamous juke box.

We took it all in, picture by picture, one by one. Rico and The One held hands and made their way to a table outside. I grabbed Plan B and followed. We sat. We talked. We laughed. And we loved our lives because California seemed like heaven that day. Rico and The One were in love and I realized that I was okay with that. My best friend was happy and his life was changing right before my eyes. He was finding that thing that we all crave deep down inside—the elusive true type of love.

The world has changed a lot since those days in California. Rico married The One and they subsequently made me move out, but best of all, I had the honor of being his best man and giving a speech at his wedding. I thought it would be cool to include it at the end of this story because it defined a period of my life where I learned and grew a lot. And we've all got friendships like this. We've all got a Rico or a Plan B that make our journeys through life a little easier. And we all owe a great deal to these people.

Life's not always a smooth ride and things don't always go as we plan. But one thing I've learned over the years is that nothing is the end of the world, that is, until it's the end of the world.

And it's not the end of the world just yet.

To Rico & The One
8-19-06

As the months leading up to today passed by at what seemed to be a steadily increasing pace, I found myself hoping that time would slow. I found myself hoping that August would somehow disappear for a while and we could go back, if only for a New York minute, to the summer of '04 when we single handedly kept most of Chicago's four AM bars in business. I found myself hoping that one of these nights I would come home to the Love Shack and see Rico standing there with that crooked grin he gets after his fifth cocktail, as laugh as he tells me how he was just kidding about all of this wedding hullabaloo.

But I don't hope this because I don't like The One or I don't like weddings or I don't like a chance to show off my sweet new dance moves to those that are rhythmically challenged. I mean, what's not to like about a beautiful woman with culinary skills that could put Emeril to shame and a chance to hear the song Butterfly Kisses for the 657th time? I say it because ever since Richie or Rico or as Wayne likes to call him "the man with the schnaz that can cause a lunar eclipse", ever since Richie looked like that little fat kid from the movie Bad Santa, and I wore hot pink Umbro shorts and oversized Phantom in-line skates, we've been best friends.

We crashed parties in our younger years and cars in our older ones, but through thick and thin, through cigarette smoke and Chicago smog and the occasional drunken wrestling match, we blazed the trails of life with a cocky swagger and an exaggerated limp. I suppose though, sifting back through memories of barn parties and that time your old man almost murdered me for swiping his bottle of Absolute vodka, that I always knew this would happen, that one day I would wake up and the mantra we had lived by our entire lives, "Bro's before ho's" would no longer ring true.

Today, it's bittersweet for me—unbelievably happy that you've finally found someone that can understand you when you start speaking in the indistinguishable vernacular that those who know you have come to expect, and a little bit like Maverick in Top Gun when Goose dies.

Seems I've finally lost my wingman.

I stand up here today, reading words that I put together and pondered over on planes and morning coffee, and know that it's impossible to reduce a lifelong friendship to a six minute speech. But I stand up here anyway, proud and honored to be your best man when I'm seated at a table of the best men. I glance at your beautiful wife and know that sometime between when you and I went to California to meet her so many weeks ago, and right now, that we've come to an agreement. That I'll step down from the role as best friend to let her resume it, as I support you from a distance while you hold her hand and tackle life's obstacles together.

I don't know how, Richie, but it seems we've gone all R&B, from boys to men. Our days of being 2 Live Crew are finally behind us and although the wheels of this ride we've been on wobble from time to time, they've yet to fall off. I love you like a brother homie, and somehow over the last year and a half, and I swear it has nothing to do with her J Lo features, I've come to love Mary too.

So with all that being said, I ask you to raise your glasses, to later on shake your asses, and toast your boy and your girl.

May your days together always be lit with the fiery conviction of romance. May your time together be long, your time apart be short, and may the best day of your past be the worst day of your future.

Congratulations.

Thoughts of a Weathered Soul

"Why did they make birds so delicate and fine as those sea swallows when the ocean can be so cruel? She is kind and very beautiful. But she can be so cruel and it comes so suddenly and such birds that fly, dipping and hunting, with their small sad voices are made too delicately for the sea"

Ernest Hemingway, The Old Man & The Sea

March, 2008

The sun has risen and set on my thirtieth birthday and I stand at the beginning of a new decade. My thoughts race, as they often do, and the uncertainties of what lie ahead have me wishing for simpler times. My hiatus from the solace I find in the simplicity of a Word document has left me with emotional baggage that is threatening to exceed my cranial weight limit, so I finally give in with hopes of purging the depths of my weathered soul.

I've gone from Chicago to Atlanta, from Atlanta to Baltimore, and from Baltimore to the beginning of a quarter life crisis. The unfamiliarity of my urban surroundings have me missing the consoling shoulders of friends that have married, gotten dogs, and begun to live out their lives by using sentences starting with "we" instead of "I." I've come to a crossroads of sorts, feeling like subject matter for a John Lee Hooker song. I feel lost in space, wondering if the clarity I was searching for in my twenties will continue to elude me through my thirties. I wonder, often so, if I will ever discover the secret of NIMH in the rat race of life.

When January came to an end I celebrated my third year of sobriety. And although I was tremendously grateful for the gifts that it has given me, I celebrated it with a deep sense of discontentment, because I feel like I have stopped evolving. My character defects seem to have resurfaced with a relentless fury as the man that I am trying to be and the man that I am seem to have reached an Old Western-esque impasse. I struggle with my own insanity lately, with the idiosyncratic nuances that comprise my uniqueness. I fight the lawlessness of a creative imagination that doesn't stay chained to the present. I fight the monumental feelings of inadequacy I have from years of being "less than" and the fallout comes in the form of a tireless and static melancholy.

In A Farewell to Arms, Ernest Hemingway wrote, "The world breaks everyone ... those that will not break it kills. It kills the very good and the very gentle and the very brave impartially. If you are none of these you can be sure it will kill you too, but there will be no special hurry."

I read his words and I don't know if I am very good or very gentle or very brave. But I do know that lately I feel trapped in the world's headlock and it's getting so very hard to breathe. My vision slowly fades as the world tightens its hold and my mind flashes back to a different time, a time where I was young and fearless and where the silver lining of life was still polished. I miss staring at my shadow on sunny summer days and pretending I was twenty-two feet tall. I miss spinning the globe and stopping it with my finger and vowing I would someday go to where it landed. I miss the scared feeling I got when I thought about holding the hand of the girl I had a crush on.

But those times have changed. Because life is constantly changing. The changing is constant. And the change that comes with the death of an entire decade has me yearning for the comforts that stability brings. So I fill my dishwasher and hang my pictures and curl up in my bed and do my best to infuse familiarity in foreign. But it's hard. Because in addition to not knowing how to navigate the City of Baltimore, I'm not quite sure how to navigate my thirties. But I will put my best foot forward and continue to walk because the world has not broken me yet.

The world has not broken me yet.

I Regret Therefore I Am

"Many of us crucify ourselves between two thieves - regret for the past and fear of the future."

Fulton Oursler

Throughout my life, I've often heard people claim that they don't have any regrets. I've heard people proclaim that they look into their pasts and find that they're at peace with who they were and what they've done.

I think they lie.

I think that because as I stare into the crystal ball and conjure up images of days that have long since passed, I see a litany of things I regret.

Like so many people in my generation, I grew up the product of a broken home. I was an angry, confused child constantly trying to find acceptance. I took long walks off short piers, leaped without looking, and even though all my friends didn't jump off of a cliff, I jumped anyway. It's been a long road just to find out that the Emerald City I'd been imagining for so long wasn't nearly as magical as I'd once hoped. I woke up from my dreams only to find out that even though last night's tornado was gone, a glance out the window revealed that another one was coming.

My dad left when I was young and, even though he had full visitation rights, he never used them. He didn't call, he didn't write, he didn't tell me to go fuck myself. He did far worse. He did nothing. I spent, no, I wasted a lot of time trying to figure out why. It didn't make any sense to me. I had tried as hard as I could to be the coolest kid I could be, to be good at everything I did, to be the Ferris Bueller and the Good Will Hunting. Ultimately, it didn't matter.

At sixteen, I called him up and asked him where he'd been. I told him it was okay, that I understood, that I didn't really care what the reasoning was behind him not being there for all those years. I told him I was a professional in-line skater, that I could do a front flip over a car, that I was sponsored, had founded my own company, and was making money putting on shows all over the Midwest. I told him all those things because in my mind, those accomplishments gave me value. They gave me validity. I felt that I had accomplished more at sixteen than most people did in their entire lives and to me that counted for something. I wasn't just a whiny kid bitching about his absentee father. I was different. I was something.

The result of that phone call was a short, sporadic and extremely one-sided relationship that did much more harm than good. He bought me a leather jacket that I didn't want or need and it was indicative of his feelings for me. It hurt like a motherfucking dagger in my back but I would never let him know. I was upset with myself for not letting sleeping dogs lie because seeing how little he cared for me hurt just as much that time as it did when I was little.

From time to time, on nights when I'm reminiscing, or days when I'm not feeling so happy, I try to find him. I Google him, hoping to find an address or a phone number so I can call and ask him, one more time, what the deal is. I guess I'm a glutton for punishment.

I think about my own struggles to be a father to Haley and I've promised to never let her feel the sting of rejection that I've felt. Being so far from her is, at times, unbearable, but I pray that she knows how much I love her and how hard I'm trying.

I don't know if I'll ever get the chance to confront my old man again and ask him all the things I've wanted to ask him. I don't know if I truly even want to. I just pray that someday I find peace and that someday he does too.

I Googled him once and found an obituary for a man with the same name. It was a strange coincidence. Although there have been a number of times that I've wished he was dead, knowing that he could be doesn't seem fair either. I don't want that opportunity to be taken away from me. For some screwed up reason, I like having the option of maybe talking to him again and if he's six feet under, I can't do that. I wouldn't be able to tell him, for the first time, that I am something.

The Fall Guys

"True friends stab you in the front."

Oscar Wilde

When I was eleven years old, I discovered that I could make a bomb by mixing hydrochloric acid and tinfoil inside of an empty two liter bottle. It was a pretty amusing way to pass the time and the explosion it gave off when it blew up resembled that of a small land mine.

There was about a year that went by in my childhood where me and the crew that I ran with terrorized the neighborhood like Hooligans after a Manchester United soccer game. We waged war against everyone over the age of twenty for an entire summer. It seemed harmless enough, and for the most part, it was until a strategically placed bomb that was supposed to take out the flower bed of old Mrs. Hinton almost blew off her left hand. She had been looking out the window when she saw us launch the fizzing two liter bottle into her flowerbed and mistakenly thought we were littering. She came barreling out her front door, yelling at us while she ran down the steps to pick up our discarded bomb. Our faces collectively turned from crimson to pale white as we all screamed in unison to put it down. There was so much yelling, her at us and us right back at her, that it wasn't until the bottle started to expand that she became aware of what was actually going on. In a panicked frenzy, she threw the almost detonated bomb back to the ground and ran up the porch steps as fast as her old legs would take her.

Seeing that Mrs. Hinton was out of harm's way, the rest of us took off down the street like we were running time trials for the Olympics. When we finally heard the explosion in the distance, and it wasn't followed by the bloodcurdling scream of someone that just lost an appendage, we decided that maybe it was time to end the war.

So end the war we did, but in the years that followed, I noticed that the feeling I got that made me want to do things like make acid bombs, or ding dong ditch the old man down the street, or throw pebbles into the backyard pool of my neighbor never seemed to go away. The restlessness that seems to only be cured by teetering the line of what's acceptable behavior nips at my heels while I continue to walk through life. And with no recess to start fights during or classes to ditch or girls to give cooties to, I've found myself staring into the face of adulthood with a gigantic pouty lip asking the question, "What can I do, excluding baggies of cocaine and drinking vodka-sevens, that can satisfy my fundamental Top Gun need?"

Well, I could jump out of an airplane.

Since the days when I was still new to the world, and trying my hardest to roll off my changing table, I've been obsessed with the thought of freefalling through the air. Fast forward through time to 1991 when Patrick Swayze and Keanu Reaves battled it out on the silver screen in the movie *Point Break* and my obsession tips the proverbial scales.

For my group of friends, the guys that constantly pushed everything to the edge, *Point Break* was a poetic expression of sheer genius. We walked around quoting its lines like they were they Bible verses.

"Fear causes hesitation and hesitation causes your worst fears to come true."

"...This was never about the money; this was about us against the system, that system that kills the human spirit. We stand for something. We are here to show those guys that are inching their way on the freeways in their metal coffins that the human spirit is still alive..."

We idolized Bohdi and Johnny Utah like some kids idolized Batman and The Man of Steel. We even went so far as to bring the movie in for our Physical Science class when we were studying the concepts of human flight and terminal velocity. We viewed the last skydive sequence where Johnny Utah jumps out of the plane without his parachute to catch Bodhi so he could rescue Tyler, but the screening was promptly shut down due to the litany of f-bombs dropped during the scene. Evidently the Chicago Christian School System didn't find the humor that we did in the term *"fuckin' A, man!"*

Yes, skydiving is one of those things that I feel like I was just born to do. The thought of being weightless and falling through the wild blue yonder at 120 miles per hour had preceded almost every attempt at jumping off my garage with an umbrella in hand when I was a kid. I knew that when I was old enough I would do whatever it took, be it beg, borrow, or steal to get myself in a plane that I could promptly jump out of.

It was during the time that I spent with The Italian Job that we had taken a vacation down to Mexico's Riviera Maya. In addition to drinking an amount of tequila that would kill a small elephant, I was finally able to fulfill my lifelong ambition to freefall. We had been walking along a crowded beach in Playa del Carmen where hordes of Mexican street merchants were trying to sell us everything from masks to marijuana. The Italian Job was doing her best to fend off the grabby little peasant kid who was trying to shake her down for a dollar when, in a moment some might call a divine revelation, I saw the sign in the distance.

Skydive. 229 US dollars.

I remember staring at the sign and feeling my heart begin to beat faster with the passing of each earthly second. It was as if the sign really said, "Tim, your destiny awaits you, come soar with the eagles."

I looked back at The Italian Job, who was down about fifteen dollars by then, and swatting at the growing number of peasant children trying to reach into her Coach bag. She managed to smack one of the kids on the top of the head and mutter some version of a Spanish cuss word and finally, she made it to where I was standing.

"I feel the need..." I said to her while pointing in the direction of the sign.

Her eyes followed my finger and I could see the panic register on her face as she began to figure out what I was referring to.

"The need for speed..." I finished the most popular line in the entire Top Gun movie with a twinkle registering ever so slightly amongst the red vessels of my bloodshot eyes.

An hour later I had paid the handsome sum of 229 US dollars and was sitting with my knees curled up to my chest in the back of a small, rickety plane as it slowly climbed the stairway to heaven. The sky was a deep blue blanket that had magically wrapped itself around our plane and the air was crisp and cool.

At ten thousand feet I tumbled out of the plane and everything that was wrong in my life, or used to be wrong in my life, or could have been wrong in my life went away. In that brief minute I felt emancipated from my mortality, devoid of my humanity, absolutely and wholly limitless.

I've often looked back on that first jump, a jump made in a time that addiction had not yet ruined, and saw it as an overture for the future. In a relatively short amount of time from that moment I would, metaphorically speaking, be spinning towards an impact with all of the things that I had been running from. I would lose everything that I had worked for—my fiancé, my job, even the integrity I had sworn to myself to uphold. But in the brief seconds that I fell towards the earth that day, I defied every restriction that was ever put on me and broke free, albeit only for a moment, from myself.

Years passed in the blink of an eye and life had changed. I was a year or so into my sobriety and I missed bits and pieces of my old life. Rico and I were still living together and for the most part, his life hadn't changed a whole lot. The Chicago nightlife still welcomed him with open arms and vodka, well, vodka was still his friend.

Rico was a pretty funny guy to be friends with and the majority of our time together was spent laughing at things we should have long since outgrown laughing at. We both still saw the humor in giving someone a "Dutch oven" and laughed anytime anyone said the word wiener. Rico was an all around good guy to be with and even though the vodka would sometimes bring out the Rico that would start fist fights with doors and walls and the occasional car window, it was only a matter of time until The Hulk would turn back into David Banner. And although his alcohol fueled valor had gotten him through a number of situations in his life that he was more than a little uncomfortable with, he had never been able to overcome his colossal fear of scary movies. He was deathly afraid of Jason and Freddy and that crazy lady from the Poltergeist movies, and while trying to tough it out through the first Candyman film in high school, I'm quite certain he suffered a mild form of heart attack.

It was always pretty funny to me see how different we were in some respects, but how similar we were in others. I found it necessary to inject adrenaline into my life on as many occasions as I possibly could, but Rico on the other hand, was fine with the snail's pace that life seemed to be moving at. And to me, this was just not acceptable.

So whenever an opportunity to get Rico out of the proverbial box that he lived in came around, that feeling I had years ago on the day that I threw that hydrochloric acid bomb onto old Mrs. Hinton's lawn would come rushing back to me like waves crashing on the beach.

A few summers after my initial skydiving adventure in Mexico, I found myself on top of a rooftop in Wrigleyville, drinking beer from a tap and taking in a Cubs game. It was a very Chicago thing to do; the rooftop that is, and while Cub fans inside the stadium left their hearts on the field after every pitch, my friends and I drank and carried on almost oblivious to the game. Cute girls in pink and white Cubs shirts served us beer and burgers while we told stories and caught buzzes. Only after the alcohol had begun to work its way into his system, did my friend Daryl finally make a confession. He had been eyeing the bartender that was serving up the drinks since we got there that morning, and he desperately wanted to talk to her.

We all sort of looked at him after he told us; me, Rico, and The Dutchman, and wondered what the freaking problem was. All he needed to do was grab her attention and let her know he was into her, maybe get her number and hook up after the game. But Daryl wasn't big on the whole "pick-up girls" thing and because, at the time, I found myself to be quite fond of the "pick-up girls" thing, I took it upon myself to make a couple of awkward introductions.

They talked that day and met up later on that evening and a mere three years later, they were getting married. It's crazy how love works sometimes. Romance over beer and baseball. Some things are just meant to be, I guess. And other things, like what this all meant to me, were almost too good to be true.

Every guy knows that the best part about watching his buddies tie the knot and merge off of life in the single lane for good can be summed up in two infamous words: bachelor party. The time honored tradition of humiliating the groom-to-be with hundred dollar wedgies and unique Sawz-all demonstrations can be the highlight of some people's year. But for us, the whole whip cream shot from a strippers boob thing had gotten somewhat old. We needed something different, something dangerous, something that would immortalize the big leap into adulthood that Daryl was going to take. So when he made the round of phone calls that would inform of us what exactly it was that we were going to be doing, I found myself rubbing my hands together while emitting a low, sinister laugh.

We were going skydiving.

Better yet, Rico was going skydiving.

I hung up the phone and looked over at Rico who was currently enamored with an HGTV television show where houses were fixed up and resold for enormous amounts of profit. I relayed the news from Daryl's phone call and watched as it began to absorb, ever so slowly, into Rico's mind. It was a bit like watching a car crash in slow motion.

In the seconds before impact the driver tries to correct his steering one last time in hopes of avoiding the crash. However, a mere instant before the collision, the drivers face contorts into an expression of sheer panic and madness, his mouth changing shape as shards of metal and glass explode all around him. Pain registers quickly and screams can be heard in far away towns.

After coming to terms with this recent revelation, Rico looked at me with a somewhat blank stare, one that was eerily reminiscent of a convicted killer accepting his death sentence. He told me that his whole life, deep down inside him, he knew that this day would come. He knew that just by being friends with me he would someday have to skydive. He wasn't all that surprised that this day had finally come, but to say the least, he was not happy about it. And by not happy, I mean in grave danger of developing a possibly fatal and extremely severe stress induced ulcer.

The days flew by, and before we knew it, the time for Daryl to say goodbye to single life was right around the corner. The Friday before the wedding, a bunch of us met at Fastest Kids house on Elston Avenue and hung out on the roof, passing out drinks and grilling. We played bean bags and talked and laughed and watched the UFC fights. Car horns continued to blow from the street below and the city was alive with activity.

About halfway through the evening Rico showed up. But he wasn't the usual Rico, he was different, concerned, vexed even. It was as if the gravity of the situation, the pending doom that awaited him the following morning had grabbed a hold of his soul and started squeezing. And so Rico did exactly what one would think he would do. He drank. He drank like the life that he cherished so dearly depended on it. He drank like it was prom night at the Drake Hotel again. He drank like the vodka was water from the fountain of youth and he was reversing a lifetime of ageing.

I watched him throughout the evening and although the drunker he got the funnier it was, I kept thinking that if there was ever two things that didn't go together very well it had to be hangovers and skydiving. But the thing about dealing with drunkenness is that logic and reasoning just won't prevail. So rather than preach to the choir, I decided to head home and get a good night's sleep before morning crept in.

I pulled up in front of Fastest Kids apartment the next morning and the first thing I saw was Rico's feet dangling off of the roof. He was chatting rapidly on the phone, his feet swinging back in forth like a child on a swing, and from the half cocked smile and slanty-eyed look he was giving me, I could tell he was a whole new kind of hungover. I ran up the stairs and into the living room where breakfast was in full swing. Fastest Kid was cooking eggs and pancakes while Daryl and the rest of the crew showered and got ready for the day. It was one of those moments where it was just good to be alive. I looked at the guys, guys that had been by my side through so much of my life and it was good to be with them. We had all grown up considerably from where we started on the Southside, but the bonds that we had formed had held strong.

I barked a few orders to get the show on the road and soon enough, with Rico and me in his A4 and Fastest Kid and Daryl on their motorcycles, we were heading down Intertate 80 without a care in the world. Hip hop poured through the speakers as the landscape changed from skyscrapers to cornfields, and an hour later we pulled up to the drop zone.

After unloading and checking in with the attendant at the counter in the front, we signed our lives away and were escorted to the plane. Rico's face had turned into a pale, gelatin like color, and we climbed aboard the plane in a single file line.

After we were all successfully seated on the floor, the pilot started the engine and we began to climb to the jump altitude of 13,500 feet. The door was open and the cool, crisp air rushed in, reminding us how real it actually was. The sky was a deep blue, a blue that seemed to engulf us the higher we flew and for the first time in our lives, we were neighbors with the clouds.

I was last to leave the plane that day and got to watch as each one of my friends jumped from the plane and into the awaiting arms of the wild blue yonder. And it was surreal. One by one they embraced their fears and dove in the unknown, throwing a middle finger towards conventional wisdom and living only for that moment. As I stood at the door of the plane, the wind howling and ripping through the calm skies with uncharacteristic ferocity, I closed my eyes and smiled, thanking God for all that he had given me, and fell from the plane.

Pay It Forward

"Dream as if you'll live forever, live as if you'll die today."

James Dean

If legend has it right, it was Benjamin Franklin who first introduced the concept of "paying it forward." This idea, known in sociology as "generalized reciprocity", was that the debtor could have the option of paying the dept *forward* to a third person rather than *back* to the original lender. In a letter to Benjamin Webb dated April 22, 1784, Franklin wrote "This is a trick of mine for doing a deal of good with a little money."

People like Ben Franklin were concerned with doing good things for other people, but people like me; people that were lost in the grasp of addiction were pretty much just interested in things like where the next party was and how we were going to get there. I was completely self-absorbed, caring only for the likes of John Barleycorn and the places that he deemed to be cool. I remember thinking that my life had somehow turned into a poorly scripted reality show. The plot was dull and repetitive and if something didn't change, it was going to be pulled off the air for good.

When the certainty of what my life had become finally set in and I was offered the opportunity to change, I boarded a plane and flew across the Midwest to the Land of 10,000 Lakes. I was going to "see a guy about a thing" but when I got there, I still wasn't quite sure who the guy was, and moreover, I was completely confused as to the identity of the thing.

I got off the plane in Minneapolis and immediately considered calling the whole thing off and getting right back on the plane. Because what no one tells you when you're getting ready to get sober is how motherfucking scary it is. Your whole life changes in an instant and the crutch that you've been using to walk your entire life is suddenly gone. You're wobbly. Everything is unsteady. You're seconds away from falling, but you know that you can't and that you've got to figure it out no matter how hard it seems.

When I got off the plane that day in January of 2005, I was met by an old man with white hair and a tan, weathered face. His eyes were kind and looked as if they had seen the best of times, and the worst of times. He knew my name. He knew why I was there and he knew how hard the next twenty-eight days were going to be. He grabbed one of my bags and side by side we walked through the airport. Busy travelers rushed by on either side of us, oblivious to the weight that I seemingly carried on my shoulders. After a bit, he stopped and looked at me, his kind eyes sizing me up, or maybe just empathizing with the fragility of my emotional state. He told me that we had one more guy to pick up and then he turned and began walking again.

We walked until we reached the gate where a plane had come in from Austin, Texas. We strolled over to a bench where a young man was sitting and the old man spoke to him. The young man on the bench was dressed all in black and had long hair, almost like Jesus in those pictures. He had a duffle bag, a guitar, and huge, imposing black eye. He was there for the same reason that I was: to get help, to find solace, to face the man in the mirror after years of trying to avoid him. We said hello, and in that moment we formed a bond. We were two broken men living in a broken world and realizing that there had to be a better, softer way.

The three of us left the airport and got into a van that was parked outside in the garage. We drove away from the city and into the country and soon we were lost in the white abyss of rural Minnesota. Snow covered evergreen trees lined the slush covered streets and I stared out the window. We didn't talk much, all of us lost in thoughts of what lie in the days ahead of us. The man with the kind eyes told us about the place that we were going, about how it would change us forever, and how we were going to get better.

I didn't believe him.

I didn't believe him, but I went anyway and at the end of my stay I was changed. I was a different person. I had some color back in my eyes and I was truly grateful to be alive.

Compared to the scandal that surrounded my departure for rehab, my emergence back into the real world was pretty uneventful. Life had continued on without me while I was away and the Chicago winds had continued to blow. But I felt different. I wanted more out of life now. I wanted more out of everything now. Rehab taught me that I had more than just a problem with cocaine and alcohol; it taught me that the way that I lived my life was fundamentally flawed. I needed to relearn how to live each day. I needed to get up on time, to make my bed, to go to bed at a decent hour, to exercise. Years of cocaine use and drinking vodka straight out of the bottle had done a number on me. Gone was the genetic gift of a washboard stomach, toned arms, and a year round tan. During the years that I had spent under the dimly lit lights of the Chicago bar scene, I had become a health and wellness statistic.

It was in rehab that I began to work out again. Most of my days were spent deep in the corridors of my mind so any chance to branch out of the therapeutic bubble I was trapped in was warmly welcomed. Hazelden housed an Olympic sized pool and a state of the art work out facility so, on more days than not, I would find myself in the gym using reps and sets to calm my animated mind.

And since rehab had, more or less, changed the way that I looked at life, I decided that I would keep up with the whole workout thing and do my best to get back in shape. As it turned out though, it wasn't quite as easy as one might have thought.

A few years earlier I had fallen victim to the crafty marketing of Bally's Total Fitness. There was a facility not too far from where my parents lived and before long, I found myself sitting at the registration desk getting suckered into a three year fitness contract. I had rationalized my decision by telling myself, in the salesman's words, that it was "an investment in my health." Which, I suppose it was, but what I failed to take into account was the fact that I hadn't ever committed to anything for three years, much less something that involved sweating and hard work. So it wasn't too long after the ink had dried on the dotted line that I had signed that I had pretty much abandoned both my workouts and the monthly payment that went along with them. And, as I soon found out, the problem with not paying your bills is that sooner or later it catches up with you.

When I began putting my life back together I had a more than a few financial amends to make. So, after what seemed like ages and ages of negotiating with the persistent bill collector that had become a staple of my morning routine due to his clockwork like calls each day, I eventually paid off the Bally's debt. And it felt good. I felt grown up and responsible and, for once, I felt like maybe the whole getting sober bit was actually paying me a few dividends.

Once the debt was satisfied, I made my way over to the Bally's Total Fitness that was housed in the basement of 230 W. Monroe

Street. And as far as gyms go, this Bally's was probably just a grade or two higher than what most people have at home in their garages. The Bally's people had somehow managed to cram a four lane lap pool, a cardio room, a dance studio, a hot tub, a weight room, two locker rooms, and nineteen treadmills in a space about the size of a tree house. It smelled like a mixture of cleaning solution, chlorine, and sweat and the equipment in it was older than I was by at least four years. It was the type of place that salesmen would say had "character" but what normal, non-salesman people would simply call "shitty." But it was perfect for me. It was perfect for me because I was fresh out of rehab and the last thing I needed was bright lights and attractive women wearing spandex (okay, maybe that part would have helped) and expensive membership dues. I just needed an escape from the reality that when I left the gym after a hard workout I was still broke, sober, and about six numbers shy of winning the lottery.

I entered the gym for the first time after I had paid off my outstanding debt and realized that I would have some explaining and/or negotiating to do with the guy in the red shirt sitting behind the reception desk. I somehow needed to convince him to let me work out there without getting locked into another contract. My rationale was this: when I signed my contract with Bally's the term was for three years. I had, in fact, paid off the bill in two years and nine months. My logic, however flawed it might have been, was that Bally's should let me workout for the remainder of my contract without having to come up with any additional funds since I had essentially fulfilled my portion of the contract.

I explained the situation to the guy working behind the desk and did my best to win him over with my argument. To his credit, he listened to me, and at one point I think I may have won him over, but at the end of my spiel, this is what he said. "Bro, it's like this. If you buy a car and you make your payments everything is all well and good. But if you decide that one day you're not going to make you're payments anymore, the bank is going to come and take away your car. You can't then waltz into the bank two years later and say you want the car back because it's gone already. And it's been gone. And that's just not the way it works. It's the same thing here, bro."

He was right, of course, but that still didn't solve my predicament. I leveled with the guy as best I could and told him part of my situation. I told him about rehab and my life recently and really just tried to do the best I could to speak the truth and hope I could appeal to his sympathetic side.

I could see him weighing the options in his head and then, with the shrug of a shoulder, he told me that he worked most of the afternoon shifts during the week and he would let me come by and work out for free.

I thanked that guy profusely and to this day I don't think he will ever fully comprehend what a huge effect that inconsequential decision of his would have on my life. It was the very definition of the butterfly effect. That one decision set in motion a sequence of events that culminated into one of the most pivotal and emotional moments of my entire life.

On January 20th, 1998 I became a father. I didn't want to be a father. I didn't know how to be a father. I was scared to be a father, but none of that mattered because on that day, while my friends studied for college tests and lived college lives, I became a father. I was a nineteen year old kid. I was a kid with a kid who couldn't kid himself into the thinking that things wouldn't change in epic ways the second she was born.

When she was finally born, when she let out her first cry and gasped for her first breath, I wept. I cried for so many reasons. I cried because I loved her the second I saw her and because she was beautiful and because her eyes were big and round and brown. I cried when I held her and when I felt her heart beat and when she looked at me. I cried while she slept and when her little hand grabbed my finger and I never, ever wanted those moments to end.

But, inevitably, those moments did end. And when they ended the tidal wave of bullshit that was threatening to crash down upon my life did so in a way that almost crushed me. My relationship with her mother went from barely tolerable to absolutely unbearable, and the criminal rap sheet I had been developing got significantly longer. I was in an out of jail and consciousness and sanity, and just a little while after my beautiful baby girl turned one, I had to make a decision. I was in Colorado. I was alone. I was getting in the type of trouble that would haunt me for years to come. I was an alcoholic, drug addicted mess. Haley's mother and I had broken up and I hated her so much that it hurt. I was homeless and slept in the back of restaurants and hostels and cheap hotel rooms. I was a complete waste of humanity, but I was still a father. And that killed me because fathers didn't do the things that I was doing. They didn't have the relationships that I had. They didn't sleep in restaurant booths and shoot guns and go to jail. And so I was faced with a decision.

I had two things I realistically felt like I could do. I could stay and continue down the road to perdition. I could continue to fight with Haley's mom and the police department and do more time and more crime until the day that something changed. That is, of course, if that day ever came. Or I could go. I could leave Haley and her mom and her sister and the motherfucking bullshit mountains. I could put my cowardly tail between my legs and go home. I could say sorry to my parents and my sisters and my brother and all the friends that I had let down and I could get on a Greyhound bus and I could go the fuck home. And I could change. I could get better and get help and try and figure out why my life had gone so tragically wrong.

Ultimately, I chose to leave. I got on a Greyhound bus with a ticket paid for by money sent Western Union from my parents and I went back to Chicago. I was so happy to be going there, to be going home, to finally be done with tragic drama of my life in Colorado. But as happy as I was at times, I was so painfully sad for leaving Haley. And not a single second has gone by since that moment that I haven't hurt because of it.

When I started my workouts again in rehab they were fueled by a maniacal insistence to quell the pain and guilt that I felt so deep inside. I wanted the wreckage of my past to dissipate into the air around me like the salty sweat that flowed from my pores. I wanted to push myself to the very edge of my limitations so the exhaustive sleep I fell into during the uneasy nights of rehab would be quiet and still and restful. I just wanted some relief, something that would make me feel a little better and a little more human and a little less like the piece of shit that I was.

The days of sobriety turned into months of sobriety, and all along the way I continued to duck in and out of the Bally's on Monroe Street. I got to know some of the people that worked out along side me and my Pinocchio-like quest of becoming a real boy again ebbed and flowed like the waves of Chicago traffic that passed outside its cold, steel doors. It slowly became my favorite part of the day. I grew to love the smell of the pool and the clutter of the hallway and the way my cell phone didn't work when I was down there. I worked out every day of the work week and on one of those days, during one of those times, I met a girl named Olivia and she was cool and fun and smart. She was a personal trainer and an aspiring actress and had a dog named Max that she loved with every beat of her strong and healthy heart. She was from Rhode Island and had come to Chicago for a weekend and never went home.

Olivia and I got along well and each day during my recess from life, in between dumbbell presses and triceps extensions and weighted push-ups, we would talk. We would talk about life and work and relationships and the impropriety of the leotard and, as time progressed, we started to talk about rehab and addiction and Haley. We would do the crossword together and little by little, day by day, week by week, we became friends. I told her about what I had gone through in the previous few years and how I was so desperately trying to rectify a situation that seemed largely irreparable. I read to her some of the things I had written for Haley and talked about my broken heart and how some days without her just seemed so sad. She listened while I talked about my financial black hole, how I was at a point where I wanted to fly to Colorado to see Haley but didn't have the money. She listened while my heart poured out feelings of inferiority and inadequacy as a father and I confessed to her that even though I was sober, I still felt like a failure. She listened and, eventually, I ran out of things to say. My workout out was over, as was my impromptu therapy session, and it was time to head home.

I went home that night to a normal routine in a life that had begun, ever so slowly, to feel normal again. I thought a lot in those early months of sobriety. I constantly evaluated and reevaluated who I was and what I was doing and tried to think of ways to right the wrongs that confronted me around every corner of Chicago's busy, city streets. I thought about Haley, about the few good memories that I had of her, and I dreamed of ways that I could get through to her, to somehow bridge the cavernous gap between us.

Life seemed to move slower back then. There wasn't the sense of urgency that accompanies one when he hits his thirties. Sobriety in the early days had of way of slowing life down in a fashion that allowed me to continually try and make the adjustments that would ensure some long term sobriety. I seemed to have more time to think, to reflect, to find the answers to some of the harder questions I had been asking.

A few days after Olivia and I had our heart to heart in the tiny office in that tiny gym off of Monroe Street, I stopped by for a workout. Olivia found me running on one of the treadmills and asked me to meet her in her office when I was through. I finished my run, cooled down for a few minutes, and casually strolled into her office. She was sitting on a chair, one of those cheap desk chairs that never seemed to balance quite right, and handed me an envelope.

I was puzzled and the look I gave her must have conveyed that I was puzzled because she told me to open it. I did. And inside was a voucher for a plane ticket. When I looked up at her, unsure, uncomfortable, and a little embarrassed by her generosity, she told me she wanted me to go see my daughter. She told me that there were some people in her life that had done some really nice things for her and she wanted to pay it forward.

I stood there on that day, in that pivotal moment in my life, and I felt something inside me change. There were good people in the world, good people that did good things that provided opportunities to people like me, people that didn't always make good decisions and good choices.

I stared at Olivia that day and felt truly blessed to have her in my life. She was a relative stranger, just another person living in Chicago and trying to make sense out of life, but she affected me in a way that was truly monumental.

I took the plane ticket from her and in the month that followed, I got on a plane. I flew to Colorado to face Haley, to tell her how sorry I was, to hold her in my arms and love her with everything I had inside me. I hadn't seen her in five years, hadn't talked with her much in the years since I had left, and felt the pain of my decision to leave with every beat of a broken heart.

Since the day that Olivia handed me that envelope we've continued to grow in our friendship together. Our lives have brought us to other cities and other circumstances, but we still manage to find enough time to catch up here and there. She gave me hope in a world that, for so long, seemed hopeless and for that I will be forever indebted to her. But as she's taught me, I won't be paying it back...I'll be paying it forward.

Oh, Canada

"Consider the past and you shall know the future."

Chinese Proverb

"Sir, as a representative of the Canadian government, I am refusing your entry into Canada."

I stood there with a blank look and tried to hide the anger that was building inside of me. Even though the words were coming out of his mouth with a brooding sense of finality, they refused to register behind the bone of my thick skull.

I pleaded.

"Sir, I am not the person I once was. I'm not the person you're seeing on those pages. Obviously I made some mistakes while I was growing up, but that was a long time ago and I've more than paid my debt to society. I've put a lot of time between the me then and the me now. Please don't do this to me."

His eyes glanced from me down to the documents and back to me. They didn't even seem angry, but there was a strong sense of resignation in them. He wasn't a man that backed down very often.

"Sir, look at these charges. Assault. Resisting arrest. Felony eluding. Burglary. Domestic violence. Criminal trespass. The list goes on and on. There are nineteen charges listed here. I cannot, nor will not, allow you to enter Canada."

I sighed audibly, exhaustedly, and looked around the room. What was I doing here in this no man's land, ostensibly stuck in the small amount of space between the United States and Canada that's apparently reserved for extensive background checks? Why was I even wasting my breath on someone who wasn't going to see things in any way other than what the black text on my rap sheet spelled out? It was an exercise in futility.

The room was brightly lit from having windows on all sides that allowed for the perfect view of both where you wanted to go, and where you came from. In the distance, the icy water roared violently over the cliffs of the Niagara Gorge before settling down in the Maid of the Mist Pool, some170 feet below. The city of Toronto looked peaceful in comparison, gazing down from its perch above the falls, alive with neon blood and casino money.

I scanned the room and settled my gaze upon the five guys huddled in the corner of the room.

I tried again.

"Sir, with all due respect, I ask you to please reconsider. I flew here this morning from Atlanta to meet those guys at the airport in Buffalo. One of my best friends is getting married and we came here to celebrate his bachelor party. Look at the dates on those charges. '97, '98, '99, 2000. I haven't been in trouble in almost eight years. That *has* to count for something."

The papers ruffled in the man's hands as he looked directly into my eyes.

"Sir, you can return to Buffalo and talk with the consulate about obtaining a pardon. If you return here with a pardon, you will be allowed to pass through. However, should you try to return through the border at any time without that pardon you will be deported, and as a result, you will never again be allowed to step foot on Canadian soil."

My heart sank into my stomach.

My cause was lost and the sooner I realized that, the better. For me, there would be no bachelor party, no afternoon limo, no hotel overlooking the mighty Niagara Falls. There would be no secrets to keep, no pacts made to cover up the results of my friends blatant inebriation, and no way to get past a past that still finds a way to punish me eight years later.

I fucking hate authority. I hate cops and rent-a-cops and Mounties and security guards. I hate jails and Customs and police stations and background checks and prosecuting attorneys. I hate the piece-of-shit public defender that convinced me to take the plea bargain that stuck me with this obtrusive felony. I hate fact that I have nineteen charges on my fucking rap sheet, but more than anything I hate fact that I am powerless to change even one of them.

The gray skies outside the building turned even grayer and the Canadian customs agent told me to meet him outside where he would give me my passport and show me how to return back to the States.

I felt like I was sixteen again, and out of all my friends I was the one with the fake ID that didn't work. I felt like the guy who goes out in downtown Chicago on Saturday night with sneakers on and can't get into the club his friends are going to. I felt like I was somehow letting everyone down, like life was laughing at me and reminding me that regardless how many Windsor knots I tie and suits I buy, no matter how many limos I ride in or how hard I work, at the end of the day I'm still me. I'm still a criminal and an alcoholic and a coke addict and a liar.

I slowly walked away from the counter and over to where Tommy and the rest of the crew were standing with apprehensive faces. I told them what was happening. I told them I couldn't go with them and I told them I was sorry. They said they understood.

I gave them each hugs; hip-hop half hugs full of attitude. I watched as they walked outside and got in their cars to leave. I watched the distance between Tommy and I get bigger and it made me sad. Tommy and I had been on different paths since I had sobered up and it hurt to watch the gap between us widen. It was hard for me to be in the same places as him. I was still battling the demons of my addictions and being in bars was a stark reminder of all the things I used to be. I had to make conscious choices to stay out of bars and house parties and events that focused around drinking because I knew if I didn't, I would slip. I would drink. And the result would be a rapid spiral downward.

I walked away and through the double doors of the building and into the parking area where my rental car was parked. The wind whipped angrily under the canopy that covered the search area. Bits of icy snow fell sideways. Canada seemed like Oz, a place that I would never be able to get to no matter how hard I tried. I was angry. Unbelievably angry. I wanted to take my rage out on Mounties and anyone else who wore a fucking uniform. I wanted to show them what a criminal really was. I wanted to go out in a blaze of glory, to hit the gas on the SUV and go out like a motherfucking gangster.

I started the car and drove over to where the customs official was waiting. He pointed in the direction of Buffalo while handing me my passport, telling me that I had to stop and check in with U.S. officials before I could get back into the states. I took my passport from his hand, rolled up the window, and drove away without saying anything. Fuck him and his high horse and his French fucking last name.

I drove the short distance to the guard shack and handed the officer my passport and paperwork. He asked me why I got refused.

I told him it was because of my criminal record. He told me to pull around the corner and park.

I slowly pulled forward and bits and pieces of my past came flooding back. I thought about the guys that I had hung out with and how a couple of them were now dead or in prison. I thought about the police chase that landed me a felony, about the gun that I used to carry with me for protection, and the kid that I jacked for eighteen dollars. I thought about the youth that I had wasted fighting an enemy that lived within.

I thought about my parents.

How were they ever going to take me serious or look at me without seeing me as the problem child I once was? How were they ever going to be proud of me when I couldn't even cross national boundaries without causing a scene? Was there ever going to be an end to the monotony of standing trial for shit that I did all those years ago?

I suppose the questions I was asking myself were rhetorical, but that didn't make them any easier to swallow. I pondered them while I waited and after a while, the customs agent came back and gave me my passport. He told me I was free to go.

I put the car in drive and drove back into Buffalo with a great sense of sadness, a definitive melancholy that always seemed to surface after a run in with my past. I was ashamed of the things I'd done all those years ago, and I desperately wanted a clean slate and another shot to make things right.

The snow began to fall lightly in upstate New York, and for a minute it seemed like the Rockies were peering down on me again with the condescending glare that I had grown so accustomed to. Things had changed, but they were still very much the same. I was still me and I always would be. I could put distance between my past and the present, but I could never outrun it. It was always there, waiting in the darkness, ready to cast shadows on my future.